20/10

# WHO'S AFRAID . . ?

# WHO'S AFRAID . . ?

## Coping with fear, anxiety and panic attacks

## Alice Neville

ARROW

Published by Arrow Books in 1991

5  7  9  10  8  6  4

© Alice Neville 1991

The right of Alice Neville to be identified as the author
of this work has been asserted by her in accordance
with the Copyright, Designs and Patents Act, 1988.

First published in 1991

Arrow Books Limited
20 Vauxhall Bridge Road, London SW1V 2SA

Random House Australia (Pty) Limited
16 Dalmore Drive, Scoresby, Victoria 3179, Australia

Random House New Zealand Limited
18 Poland Road, Glenfield
Auckland 10, New Zealand

Random House South Africa (Pty) Limited
Endulini, 5a Jubilee Road, Parktown 2193, South Africa

RANDOM HOUSE UK Limited Reg. No. 954009

A CIP catalogue record for this book
is available from the British Library

Papers used by Random House UK Limited
are natural, recyclable products made from wood grown in
sustainable forests. The manufacturing processes conform to
the environmental regulations of the country of origin

ISBN 0 09 984970 4

Phototypeset by Intype, London
Printed and bound in Great Britain by
Cox & Wyman Ltd, Reading, Berkshire

*To Michael*

*I would like to thank Dr Claire Weekes'*
*publishers, Angus and Robertson, for their*
*permission to quote from Dr Weekes' book*
Self-Help for your Nerves.

# CONTENTS

# FOREWORD

It is twenty-five years since I started the first agoraphobia self-help organization – The Open Door – which had around 30,000 members during the ten years in which I was involved with it. The following ten years I spent bringing up my family and working as a curator in the National Maritime Museum in Greenwich. After writing two books about Louis XIV and Nelson, I wrote *Who's Afraid of Agoraphobia?* in 1986 and once again I was involved. Hundreds of sufferers contacted me, along with many other people who found that they could identify with the problems agoraphobes had, but did not consider themselves truly agoraphobic. Most admitted that they suffered from general anxiety, panic attacks or obsessive-compulsive disorders.

A new information service I set up to help agoraphobia sufferers was to become PAX (Panic Attacks and Anxiety), to cover a much broader spectrum including all the above problems.

This book could never have been written without the help of former Open Door members and present PAX contacts. Some of the experiences quoted throughout the book were told to me by these people and others are my own experiences, from when I had these problems myself over thirty years ago.

I recovered from my agoraphobia and I shed all the anxieties and fears that had been part of my life from the age of seven to twenty-seven. I know many many other people who have also made a good recovery. I also know that although great progress has been made in treating anxiety disorders, treatment is not available to many anxiety sufferers for a variety of reasons so the emphasis of this book is on self-help.

PAX provides information on treatment through regular newsletters, and contact with self-help groups and other phobia organizations. Organizations like PAX and some of the others listed in the back of this book change and develop all the time, so please don't hesitate to contact me directly for up-to-date information.

> PAX *is the Latin word for Peace. I hope this book will bring you peace of mind.*

Alice Neville

The feminine pronoun is used most of the time, simply because a great many of my contacts are women. I am not ignoring the fact that men are sufferers, too, and use 'he' or 'him' when appropriate.

# INTRODUCTION

It is estimated that in the UK around two million people are receiving treatment for agoraphobia. But this figure is based on the number of those who have actually sought specialist help. In 1990 a report by the Royal College of Psychiatrists stated that more than nine million Britons will suffer from abnormal anxiety and fears at some time in their lives. Such anxieties include phobias, sudden and unexpected attacks of panic, and continuous worry that something unexpected is just round the corner.

'These feelings can have a profound and detrimental effect on a person's life,' says the chairman of the college's public education committee, Professor Brice Pitt. 'We believe there is a need for the public to understand that anxiety and phobias are common and can be explained in terms of the normal workings of the body. There are also many ways of helping people who suffer from these conditions.'

There is a vast army of sufferers struggling on alone trying to live with their nervous problems and reluctant to admit them. All too frequently, when they do confide in their GPs they get very little in the way of help as long as they appear to be maintaining a normal life.

Among the hundreds of letters received after recent television documentaries, eighty per cent were from agoraphobia sufferers and the rest were from others whose phobias ranged from cows to cotton wool, and from false teeth to funerals. 'This is ruining my life' was the message. Very few of them were able to get treatment for their phobias, nor did they receive much sympathy from their families and friends.

Anxiety is the constant companion to so many of us. The Latin word *anxius* meant 'to press tightly or to strangle'. The dictionary defines it as a state of chronic apprehension. There are many types of anxiety, as we shall see, but an important fact is that anxious people invariably have over-active imaginations and constantly project their thoughts into the future, anticipating what *might* happen rather than what *will* happen. Too often anxiety develops into a chronic condition where the sufferer is afraid of the anxiety itself and is then caught in a vicious circle which is very difficult to break.

Many of those with anxiety problems never seek advice, fearing that their doctors might be unsympathetic or, worse, that they may be referred to a psychiatric hospital and labelled 'mentally ill'. They prefer to suffer in silence, ignorant of other alternatives and reluctant to seek professional help.

Some people are naturally timid, going through life trying to avoid confrontations and situations that they feel might upset their equilibrium. Rude behaviour from a stranger or a family row will upset them for days and they will avoid arguments at all costs. It is now accepted that many of us are born with a pre-disposition towards anxiety; others, as we shall see later in the book, may become over-sensitized as a result of some traumatic event – physiological or psychological – and find that they can not cope with the stresses of everyday life.

In an over-sensitized state, these people may experience chronic, nagging anxiety which can disrupt their lifestyles or, in more severe cases, become overwhelmed by sudden devastating attacks of acute anxiety, commonly called panic attacks.

Driving along the motorway at around sixty miles an hour, I thought I must have been in an accident and died, the sensation was so weird and out of this world. After the first flash I managed to drive on to the hard shoulder and pull up. By that time I was shaking violently, sweat was pouring from me and I felt as though a great weight was pressing on me, stopping me from breathing. It was no accident, I realized, but by then I was convinced I was having a heart attack. There was no way I could get out of the car to get help and I just sat there trying to make sense of the totally unreal feelings. After some five minutes things began to get back to normal and I nervously started the car and crept along cautiously, hoping I would reach the next exit safely. Once off the motorway I felt all right and eventually got home.

When I saw my doctor and underwent various tests he told me I had experienced an acute panic attack, probably due to recent stresses at home and in the office. I am a professional man in my forties and consider myself pretty well balanced. This episode has shaken me badly. I'm still not sure why it happened and can't help worrying about it happening again.

This is a description of a 'typical panic attack'. Although it is generally assumed that there is always a trigger, this is not always the case. Panic attacks can strike without warning, when the subject is feeling entirely normal. On the other hand, attacks can start with recognizable feelings of apprehension and anxiety that swiftly build up until the sufferer feels the situation getting out of control.

A panic attack is not dangerous in itself, but *fear of the fear* can literally ruin someone's life. Agoraphobia may start when a panic attack strikes in a specific situation. The situation itself becomes the focus of the fear because the subject expects a repetition of the original panic attack and, anticipating it, inevitably triggers it off. For example, the gentleman in the above example may begin to associate his panic with motorways, eventually avoiding them altogether in an attempt to avoid a repeat attack. But the motorway was not the *cause*.

'If I avoid the situation, I may avoid the panic attack' is the reasoning. But when it does recur, in a new situation, it means that there is yet another place or activity to avoid. Trying to avoid the fear means avoiding the situation where it occurs and this soon becomes a habit – the habit of agoraphobia. Unfortunately, the habit grows until more and more situations become 'hostile' and the sufferer retreats further until only in her home can she feel safe from the terrifying sensations. This is the 'typical' agoraphobia syndrome. Unchecked, fears *can* lead to such feelings.

Phobias are not a phenomenon of contemporary life; through

the ages people have suffered from a variety of phobias, but it is interesting to find that there are few historical references to women being affected. This does not mean that women did not suffer from them, but probably reflects the sexist bias that only events happening to men are worth recording!

A notable exception was Maria de Medici. Although she loved flowers she could not bear roses and felt faint if she saw one, even in a painting.

Apparently, there was no shame attached to a man admitting to a specific phobia, but when agoraphobia – with its background of sudden panic attacks – became recognized it quickly came to be considered a woman's problem. Described until recently as the 'housebound housewife's complaint', or the 'empty nest syndrome', it was linked with menopausal women whose children had left home. It was assumed that these women's husbands had better things to do than foster such neurotic behaviour as the women sat at home anxious and bored, with little to do but to brood over imaginary symptoms.

This is a very out-of-date and dangerous concept, but the stigma still persists and it is little wonder that many agoraphobic men dislike being identified with the condition.

It must be said that not *all* agoraphobia sufferers experience constant panic attacks. Some women may become housebound for a variety of reasons, resulting in a loss of confidence and avoidance of leaving the house. The longer this lasts, the more nervous the subject becomes as the outside world appears hostile and threatening. If she is persuaded to go further than her base she may well experience rising anxiety leading to a full-blown panic attack.

There are many examples during the last hundred years or so of women who were quite possibly suffering from what we would now call agoraphobia. Shock, anxiety, frustration and physical ill-health often lie behind the development of agoraphobic symptoms. How many swooning Victorian matrons languished on their day-beds? How many wilting maidens suffered fits of 'vapours' or slipped into a decline that might today be recognized as agoraphobia?

In later life, Florence Nightingale, with no physical outlet for her tremendous nervous energy, became housebound and was a semi-invalid for many years. After the shock of Prince Albert's death, Queen Victoria retreated from public life, unable to face her subjects *en masse*. Elizabeth Barrett was confined to her couch with physical symptoms which miraculously improved after Robert Browning whisked her off to Italy and married her. Retrospectively we can only guess, but each of these ladies displayed classic agoraphobic tendencies.

There are, of course, a few recorded incidences of male agoraphobes. Sigmund Freud, though not strictly agoraphobic, had a pathological fear of travelling which is a feature of the condition. He would become so anxious that he would arrive at a station at least an hour before his train was due to leave.

A professor of English at Cambridge suffered from agoraphobia for forty-eight years, managing to hide this from colleagues and students and never seeking medical help. Only his family and close friends knew of his condition, though it may well have been noted by others that the only way he could cross the college quadrangle was by sidling round the sides with his back to the wall.

An American professor wrote in 1928:

Let me assume that I am walking down University Drive by the Lake. I am a normal man for the first quarter of a mile; for the next hundred yards I am in a mild state of dread, controllable and controlled; for the next twenty yards in an acute state of dread, yet controlled; for the next ten, in an anguish of terror that hasn't reached the crisis of explosion; and in a half dozen steps more I am in as fierce a panic of isolation from help and home and of immediate death as a man overboard in mid-Atlantic or on a window ledge far up in a sky-scraper with flames lapping his shoulders.

It is as scientific a fact as any I know that my phobic seizures at their worst approach any limits of terror that the human mind is capable of in the actual presence of death in its most horrible forms.

By the Twenties, it was accepted that many women suffered from 'nervous debility', brought on by the stresses and strains of the post-war era. It was, however, assumed that the 'lower classes' did not suffer from these problems, lacking the refinement and delicate sensibilities of the middle-class housewife who, for the first time, was having to cope without cook, housemaid, nanny, dressmaker and other household staff. The magazines of the time are full of letters from ladies suffering from shattered nerves, who could no longer withdraw into a state of genteel ill-health, but had to run their households and look after their families single-handed.

'Life is moving too fast for many of us,' wrote the editor of *Woman*. 'We are all having to cope with the pace of modern living.'

Well, life is moving a great deal faster, some seventy years later, and we know that many women from all walks of life are finding it difficult to handle the emotional problems brought on by the stresses and strains of life today. Apart from domestic worries, we are forced to face up to employment difficulties, and to the disasters that are occurring throughout the world – war, famine, AIDS and other health hazards, global warming, etc. Even those who become housebound cannot distance themselves from the outside world today, and little is being done to help them face up to and cope with their fears.

The majority of sufferers can pinpoint the onset of panic attacks and agoraphobia, whether they developed over a period of years or suddenly struck out of the blue. An accident, operation or childbirth; an emotional shock, bereavement, a prolonged period of stress – all these can lead to a sensitized nervous state which in certain individuals will ultimately develop into something more serious. Eventually, the original cause ceases to matter; the agoraphobic person becomes trapped – not by earlier traumas, stresses or strains, but by sheer habit. She has so conditioned herself to feeling bad in certain situations that the outcome is inevitable if she happens to find herself thus 'trapped'. So what happens? She avoids them at all costs. Some long-term agoraphobics may not even be able to recall the last time they experienced a full-blown panic attack, but – trapped by the *fear* of fear – they are not prepared to risk facing a dreaded situation, 'just in case'.

# INTRODUCTION

People may experience anxiety attacks in all sorts of situations and at any time. The sensations associated with acute anxiety are so similar to many physiological disorders that sufferers are convinced that they are experiencing a heart attack, a stroke or other serious illness. I hope that this book will help to put many minds at rest, and to encourage sufferers to take the first steps to helping themselves to overcome their nervous problems. You *can* help yourself. It used to be thought dangerous to concentrate on overcoming phobias and panic attacks without tackling underlying psychological problems with the help of an expert. We now know that that is not usually the case. This is the era of self-help, and I hope that you will be able to put into practice many of the suggestions you will read about here.

# 1
# UNDERSTANDING YOUR FEARS

Fears, phobias, panic attacks, anxiety. How on earth do we sort out which is which and where one takes over from another? The Old English word *faer* meant 'sudden danger', and fear is what we experience when something dangerous or unpleasant is happening to us. Fear is immediate. Without any conscious effort our body reacts by producing the sensations which we often interpret as equally as unpleasant as the cause.

Our forebears had good reason to be fearful. In order to survive, it was necessary for man to be continually on the alert for danger. Marauding tribes and dangerous animals on the prowl were a constant threat when you had only a club for a weapon and the sparse shelter of a cave to retreat to.

When danger threatens, the human body prepares for action as its anxiety response triggers off nervous chemical reactions. The heart beats faster, blood is shifted from other areas to limb muscles and to the brain, encouraging quick thinking and vigorous activity. Our cave man, his survival at risk, would be 'tensed up' and ready for action – to stand and fight or to run for his life.

Over the centuries, as man has become more or less civilized, survival has become easier and most of the earlier dangers have disappeared. Of course modern man has his problems – mainly of his own making – but apart from those people for whom danger is a normal way of life, either in their profession or for entertainment, most of us are fairly assured of our survival to a ripe old age, bar accident or illness. The danger response is not now a necessary daily part of our bodily functions, so when it does occur it is likely to have longer-lasting disturbing effects.

The cave man, victorious in battle or having escaped from a woolly mammoth or a sabre-tooth tiger for the umpteenth time would relax and sleep by his fire, forgetting his nerve-racking experience until the next time. Nowadays, the emotional consequences of a bad shock or accident will persist for much longer and, being unused to such experiences, we resent the effect they have on our wellbeing.

Not everyone experiences an adrenalin boost when faced with sudden fear. Certain animals will 'freeze', roll themselves into a ball or pretend to be dead – 'playing possum' – and some humans may also find themselves inexplicably rooted to the spot, rigid with fear and so tense they feel virtually paralysed. Understandably this situation frightens them even more.

There are people who *enjoy* the physical sensations of fear and who deliberately expose themselves to dangerous situations, frequently seeking a hobby or career where there is an element of danger, and indulging in hair-raising activities in the name of sport, adventure or exploration. Many of us are ashamed to admit that we might be nervous or fearful, since courage has always been considered to be a superior virtue. From childhood we have been told to be brave and not to show fear.

A certain amount of fear is healthy, and it prevents us from risking ourselves in dangerous situations. There are, however, many of us who, because of our personalities, are more prone to fear than others. We can all understand being terrified when confronted with a dangerous situation, though, in these days, apart from being attacked by a mugger or injured in a car accident, life isn't all that dangerous. If we *are* faced with a life-threatening situation, however, the 'flight or fight' response that our cave man experienced is perfectly normal. In fact, it is imperative that our automatic system goes into overdrive in order that we may tackle the emergency or retreat from the scene as quickly as possible. But sometimes we get the wrong signals. A sudden surge of fear, even when no danger exists, causes bodily changes. Adrenalin pours into the system, the body prepares itself for action . . . but no action follows. If the nervous energy could be discharged, the body would settle down. But when this does not happen there is physiological confusion. I'm sure you recognize the sensations: racing heart, dry mouth, clammy hands, over-breathing, dizziness, a 'tight band' round the head, vision disturbance, a 'lump' in the throat, buzzing in the ears. The feelings build up until they seem unbearable, and the sufferer, clinging to the nearest static object to support her 'jelly legs' thinks 'I can't stand it. My system won't take any more. I'll have a heart attack, a stroke, a burst blood vessel. I'll drop down dead, I know I will . . .'.

The Ancient Greeks believed that Phobos, the god of fear, could strike terror into the hearts of his victims, causing them to flee blindly into the clutches of Pan, the god with the ability to induce a state of uncontrolled behaviour in men and animals . . . a state of 'panic'. This is why we call the experience of the sensations described above a *panic attack*.

The panic element arises because the subject feels out of control. It is possible to experience acute anxiety without the panic, the out-of-control sensation – in fact, I would suggest that the majority of 'panic' attacks would be better described as acute anxiety attacks because there isn't that extra nightmare dimension.

The first time in my life that I recognized a state of panic was when my pony bolted with me along a country lane and out into the main road. It seemed inevitable that we were going to be involved in a dreadful accident. My right foot was caught in the stirrup and I was holding on round the pony's neck. I hadn't enough breath to scream and felt as though the whole thing was happening to someone else. Luckily, my foot slipped free and I fell on to the road as the pony stopped.

A few months later I was walking near this scene. I was still a young teenager and hadn't a care in the world but suddenly I experienced the same feelings that I had had when on that terrifying ride. The experience was so awful I really panicked. Heading for home, I ran as fast as I could. But the feelings got worse, I did not know where I was, there was a red haze spinning round me. I saw two middle-aged women I knew slightly and asked them to help –

but I could not explain what was wrong. I sat on a grassy bank by the country road and the women hovered over me, concerned but perplexed. Each time I stood up and tried to walk, the unreal feelings got worse. Eventually I reached home and began to feel more normal. I made up some sort of excuse as I thanked my companions for their help. I never went near those crossroads again.

Many years later, I experienced the same sensations when, after a series of operations, I suffered from agoraphobia for a period of five years. An anxiety state was diagnosed and treated by a sympathetic GP, but even he could not explain the acute panic attacks that seemed to come out of the blue.

This woman's experiences are typical of many who suffer from panic attacks. The original incident is never forgotten and though, in some cases, the acute panic attack is never repeated, the memory is there in the background. Until this spectre is confronted and banished it will always be a barrier to recovery. The following story is typical and I have heard it told in slightly different ways over and over again:

I had worked hard throughout the school year and was devastated when struck by a viral infection a few weeks before my A-level exams. I worried myself sick in case I was not fit enough to sit the exams but, in fact, I recovered in time and did much better than I had expected.

I was euphoric at the prize-giving ceremony at the end of term, relieved at having done well, relieved that the period of intensive study was over, and excited at the prospect of a holiday abroad.

Halfway through the speeches I began to feel as though I was going under an anaesthetic. I saw everything through a haze; the speaker's voice sounded strange and indistinct; I was in a nightmare world where nothing seemed real. I had to get out before something terrible happened and I pushed my way to the end of the row and fled from the hall. Once outside I immediately felt better and though I was shocked at having made such an exhibition of myself, the staff and all my friends were sympathetic and the incident was soon forgotten.

I have never had a recurrence of that panic attack but to this day I cannot sit for long in church and am wary of large functions in case I am 'trapped'. I only feel at ease when I am near an exit and at the end of a row.

In this and many other cases it is the expectation of a panic attack, or the '*fear of the fear*' that is so crippling.

It is difficult to believe that there will not be some frightful climax to a panic attack but, in fact, these feelings can only reach a certain level and then they gradually subside. This does not mean that there are no after-effects of such an experience. A severe panic attack can leave you in a highly sensitized state – weak and exhausted – but it cannot damage you physically.

'I am terrified I am going to faint' is a common fear. Many people truly believe that a loss of consciousness must be inevitable whilst suffering an attack. Some experts interpret this as the patient's horror of drawing attention to themselves, but in reality it is more often fearing the loss of control with no possibility of returning to normal.

UNLESS YOU HAVE ALWAYS BEEN A 'FAINTER' YOU WON'T FAINT.

In the last century women swooned frequently in order to escape from a situation they could not face up to. Nowadays we rarely employ this means of escape! Where there is a nervous 'collapse' it is usually a conscious act that gets one out of the situation as quickly as possible – onlookers will generally rally round and offer sympathetic help. An ambulance will whisk the unfortunate sufferer off to hospital where, after a barrage of tests, the episode is diagnosed as an acute anxiety attack.

It is the need to break out of the vicious circle of fear/panic/fear that might cause someone to seek help in this way, by drawing public attention to themselves. Alternatively, they might genuinely think they are suffering from a heart attack. Unlike a typical hypochondriac who needs to draw attention to herself, the anxiety sufferer usually hates to be 'exposed', but there is often no way out.

Casualty departments are experienced in these types of emergencies, which happen all the time, and hospital staff are always sympathetic. Such symptoms cannot be ignored because there just might be a physical reason for them, and nobody can blame a patient for feeling ill. Usually the sufferer is advised to go back to her GP. But, miserable and still very frightened, she is unlikely to be reassured. From then on, always at the back of her mind is the question, 'What if it happens again?'

This is known as *anticipatory anxiety*, the gnawing, persistent worry that dominates the lives of so many of us. One fictional character demonstrates a good example of anticipatory anxiety. This is the White Queen in Lewis Carroll's *Through the Looking Glass*. She upset Alice by screaming hysterically, expecting at any moment to prick her finger. When her brooch slips and stabs her she makes an immediate recovery. ' "That accounts for the bleeding you see," she said to Alice with a smile. "Now you understand the way things happen here."

' "But why don't you scream *now*?" Alice asked, holding her hands ready to put over her ears again.

' "Why, I've done all the screaming already," said the Queen.'

Usually the agony of anticipation is far, far worse than the expected event – which may not even happen.

People who have over-active imaginations are permanently bothered by anticipatory anxiety. Their thoughts jump ahead as they see only too clearly the result – or what they *think* the result will be – of every move they make.

You know what I mean. How many times when your child has been late home have you actually visualized yourself attending his funeral? Your husband hasn't telephoned . . . he must have had a heart attack or crashed the car. (Or be wining and dining another woman?) Why hasn't your daughter telephoned? She's run off with that dreadful young man or, worse still, been abducted. You have been away from home for a few days and when you return and turn into your road . . . surprise, surprise . . . your house is still standing, though you had almost resigned yourself to finding it a burnt-out shell.

Calamity syndrome is the name of this out-of-control imaginative activity and things get to a stage where the sufferer cannot bear to be out of her home or parted from her family because she can see only disaster. This fear of being parted from things in anticipation of danger is also known as *separation anxiety*.

I am only at ease when my family is around me. From the time my husband leaves for work and the children are at school I worry about what might be happening to them. Holidays I dread as I am not happy being away from home in case something dreadful happens or something might prevent us returning in one piece.

I feel I may have acquired this tendency from my mother who constantly reminded me that the outside world was a dangerous place.

The separation anxiety experienced by this sufferer has reached the point where it affects her day-to-day activities and she is experiencing agoraphobic inclinations. She is afraid of being separated from her family and her home. Less focussed anxiety, when we are generally fearful and ill-at-ease, but cannot identify the cause, is called *free-floating anxiety* where the threat is coming from inside ourselves as much as from outside. Free-floating anxiety becomes very difficult to cope with because we feel we need an explanation for our fears; there must be a reason for the continual anxiety. This is often when a phobia develops. We fix our fears on to a specific object or situation and feel that if we can avoid it we will be able to fend off the anxiety that it causes.

There are, of course, degrees of fear, and people are inclined to declare that they have a phobia when they really mean that they have a dislike of something. On a television programme recently the presenter said that there were 'mild phobias and severe phobias'. How misleading that statement was. There is no such thing as a 'mild' phobia. Someone suffering *phobic anxiety* is suffering from a fear which is severe enough to alter or seriously disturb her life. The object of the fear, or the situation in which she experiences irrational fear, must be avoided at all costs. Consider these examples of different people's attitudes:

I have always had a dread of visiting the dentist and put off making an appointment as long as possible – usually when I have a problem! My dentist is always sympathetic. 'How's the dental phobia today?' he says and I laugh with him – albeit somewhat nervously. I am relieved when the treatment is completed and promise that I will make the next appointment on time. I know many people have a dentist phobia but I would like to get over mine.

Think that's a dental phobia? Try this:

The very thought of having to go to the dentist makes me feel physically sick. In fact, I go out of my way to avoid the dental surgery, walking a longer way round to the shops. I am terrified of seeing a dental surgery on television or reading in the newspapers about a dentist.

I lie awake at night worrying about my teeth; a little twinge makes me panic in case pain-killers have lost their effect. I've heard of people like me pulling out their own teeth when the pain got too much to bear and this makes me even more frightened.

I've asked my GP, but he isn't too concerned and says I should have intravenous valium to put me right out. He doesn't understand that I couldn't walk into the dentist's surgery in the first place. Life is a misery with this hanging over me all the time.

Those who light-heartedly bandy the word 'phobia' around do not appreciate that this is a condition severe enough to seriously disrupt the sufferer's life. The object of the fear, or the situation in which the person experiences irrational fear, has to be avoided at all costs. Many *specific* phobias are of animals, but virtually anything can become the object of someone's phobia. We will look at phobias in general in Chapter 8, but here we will concentrate on one, or rather the multiple phobias that make up the most complicated and disruptive phobia of all – agoraphobia.

# AGORAPHOBIA

The Greeks had a word for it – *agora*, the place of assembly, and *phobos*, terror or flight. The term agoraphobia, however, was not used until the late nineteenth century when a German psychiatrist named Westphal described 'the impossibility of walking through certain streets or squares or the possibility of so doing only with resultant dread of anxiety'. Flight is the key part of the word's root. When panic strikes, the overwhelming need is to escape. If you are out in the open you must get under cover; if you are in a confined space you look around wildly for an exit. You must get away from the people milling about you, must escape from the noise, the silence, the bright lights, the darkness. There are so many things to dread and all of them contradict each other. No wonder the sufferer is confused to be told that agoraphobia – traditionally held as a fear of open spaces – is the problem when she feels just as panic-stricken in a lift or hemmed in by a crowd. Isn't this *claustrophobia*?

The definitions of the two states may appear to be contradictory but agoraphobia and claustrophobia both apply to a state of anxiety which manifests itself in certain situations, causing feelings of panic and a need to escape from and avoid these situations.

*Trapped*! Inside or out the feelings are the same.

Thousands of people who would call themselves normal and well balanced, otherwise untroubled by any nervous problem, will admit freely to sensations of mild claustrophobia in certain situations. For some reason this is quite OK – claustrophobia is a socially acceptable problem as it does not usually have a devastating effect on the sufferer's lifestyle. It is accepted with tolerance, by the majority of people who can identify with it and who will suggest the obvious solution – avoid that situation.

The agoraphobe's dilemma is that if she experiences these feelings in certain situations she will avoid those places in order to avert the panic. But with sensations of anxiety always present she then begins to worry about other situations. She expects the panic to occur – so inevitably it does, almost as though her mind has an 'on' switch which operates whenever she thinks about the dreaded place. The trouble is that she does not know how to operate the 'off' switch, so she retreats to safety. Only soon nowhere is safe. If she is really unlucky she will eventually feel that the only place to escape panic is behind her own front door; but even then, if the habit of switching on fear has become established, the security of her own home may not protect her from the dreaded attacks.

# Unreality

Most people who suffer from acute anxiety have experienced the terrifying feeling of unreality that can suddenly arise, or, in some cases, hover constantly just below the surface.

In the medical material available on the subject, very frightening feelings and emotions are labelled, and neatly pigeon-holed. Very obviously the writers have never experienced any of these feelings themselves. Words like 'depersonalization' and 'derealization' do not describe the sensations and can be unnerving for the sufferer, who is trying to find an explanation. Inevitably the following extract, from *Harper and Roth Comparative Psychiatry*, is quoted in every book about phobias:

> The patient feels temporarily strange, disembodied, cut off or far away from her immediate surroundings, or feels that some change has occurred in her environment. The change referred to herself is called depersonalization, while the same change referred to her surroundings is called derealization . . . temporary phasic phenomena which last a few seconds, minutes or several hours.
>
> Its onset and termination are generally abrupt . . . the onset can follow some situation of extreme anxiety.

What a frightening and confusing description. Personally, I could not sort out depersonalization from derealization. *Everything* was unreal during a bad panic attack.

You feel that you are unique in such a situation, that no one has ever felt quite so awful. When undergoing a particularly bad attack you may feel as though you are in a nightmare, you are walking but not moving, voices and other sounds have a disembodied quality and your eyes play tricks as buildings appear to lean towards you. There seems to be no way back to normality and you feel that perhaps there never will be a way back, that you are stuck in an unreal limbo forever.

Unless someone has experienced these sensations it is difficult to understand what it is like. Even those close to you cannot comprehend your fears, and patients in treatment are often disappointed by their therapists' inability to explain what is wrong and how to handle it.

Psychiatrists tell us that depersonalization is a cut-off mechanism which is triggered when anxiety reaches a certain level. Although it is unpleasant and frightening, it is really a sort of defence, we are assured. The mind switches off when it becomes overloaded. It is easy to think that this may be the onset of a serious mental disorder but I promise you that it is not. When I was a teenager – and reading every medical book I could lay my hands on to try and discover what was wrong with me – I decided that my 'funny turns' were some sort of epileptic episode and for years I convinced myself that I was suffering from such a serious illness that the adults dared not tell me what was wrong.

You may know of a mentally ill person who suffers from acute anxiety attacks but just because the symptoms are similar to those which you experience does not mean you are suffering from *their* disorder. Anxiety and panic attacks can strike anyone, particularly if they are highly strung and over-sensitive.

'But I do not suffer from phobias or panic attacks,' you may say. 'I am just generally nervy and rather fearful!' You are probably reading this book to see if you are heading for a nervous breakdown. It is much more likely that your fears and increasing anxieties are caused by nervous exhaustion which in turn leads to loss of confidence and fearfulness. I know that many people are afraid to read books about fears and phobias; and, those who are over-sensitive feel they might 'pick up' other people's symptoms.

Once you learn that you are not totally powerless to help yourself you will have overcome the first hurdle towards recovery – whether you are suffering from a long-held fear, a new series of panic-attack situations or just general anxiety. Knowing that so many men and women share your feelings might help you accept that *any* kind of fear or anxiety is normal and, most important, curable – by you on your own, or with the help of a friend, GP, support group or therapist.

# 2
# THEORIES AND THERAPIES

## HOW DOES IT START?

Some phobias seem literally to come from nowhere, for no reason. Others gradually build up over the years from being a relatively minor fear to a life-disrupting terror.

A 'simple' phobia is an isolated fear of a single object or situation, a fear that is irrational, excessive and life-altering. You might think that the phobic person becomes anxious only when exposed to the object of their phobia or the situation in which they feel distress, but a true phobia affects the sufferer *all the time* as their mind is continually concerned with the problem: A serious sufferer may live with it every moment of the day and often can think of little else.

This is what distinguishes a phobia from the sort of fear most people experience. You can be terrified of snakes if you see one, but in this country it is an unlikely occurrence unless you go to the zoo. The phobic person will worry about snakes every day of his life, will avoid looking at a book in case there is a picture of a snake, never watch wildlife programmes on the television, will dream about snakes and allow his imagination to run riot, conjuring up thoughts of the dreaded creature until he feels that the phobia is dominating his entire life, and bringing with it a continual state of anxiety with all its unpleasant sensations.

Many people will tell you that they have a phobia, but although they may certainly have a problem, most will be able to put it out of their minds unless suddenly confronted with the object of their fear.

What *is* different from fear of this kind is chronic anxiety,

31

from which roughly five per cent of the population suffer. They are born predisposed to anxiety and will probably always have nervous problems. Sometimes the anxiety bubbles up and because there is no apparent cause the sufferer will subconsciously harness it to an object or situation. All the underlying anxiety is concentrated on this object which will, for some reason, trigger off even more anxiety. Basically, this is a fear of fear.

This is very clear in the case of situational phobias. If a panic attack strikes when someone is in a certain situation it comes to be identified with that situation and the sufferer expects it to recur. She will avoid the situation . . . just in case. Because she waits for panic to strike again it does.

Understanding our fears is the key to beating them – the powerlessness and incomprehension that anxiety fosters can be alleviated through self-knowledge.

## Psychological Reasons

For years it was believed that there had to be a psychological reason for phobias. Freud published an important case study about a five-year-old boy who was frightened of horses. Freud decided that little Hans's guilt about sexual feelings towards his mother made him afraid that his father would castrate him for having such wicked thoughts, thereby turning him into a girl. Because this fear was so great Hans deliberately put it out of his mind and displaced his anxious feelings for his father with something more neutral – horses. Being afraid of horses protected him from the conscious fear of his father and he could more easily avoid horses than the father they symbolized. So the internal danger (the fearsome father) was transformed into an external danger (the biting horse). Neurotic anxiety arising out of the original conflict of loving and envying is turned into a more acceptable anxiety about a specific animal.

Other reasons for phobias were later postulated by Freud and his followers, the unconscious fears expressing themselves in a symbolic manner as a phobia. For example, if a child is school phobic he may have an unconscious fear of killing his mother; or a fear of crowds may arise from a desire to exhibit oneself.

Early theories about agoraphobia revealed the street as a symbolic opportunity for sexual adventures. This idea still persists in some countries today where agoraphobia is known as the 'latent prostitute syndrome'.

Today, Freudians feel that even adult non-sexual sources of anxiety may produce phobias, but the important point is that the subject must remain unaware of the source of his anxiety. It is reasonable to think that someone would rather fear something specific and definite than experience free-floating anxiety, where he has no idea of the reason for his fear. Converting anxiety into a concrete fear we can cope with is preferable to the unknown.

Analytical psychotherapists feel that phobia sufferers must not learn to face up to their present fears but be encouraged to see the deeper meaning behind them so that emotional conflicts and weakness of long-standing phobias are brought into the light of day and dealt with. 'This goes to the heart of the trouble, to the point from which any radical cure must begin,' said Muriel Frampton in *Agoraphobia: Coping With the World Outside*. 'The trained psychotherapist explains or interprets the patient's feelings and demonstrates how they came to be experienced and why they caused such intense anxiety. This makes it possible for the patients to replace the negative emotions with the positive motivation which makes for wholeness.'

Ten per cent of the original Open Door members – the wealthier ones – had been undergoing psychoanalysis in the hope that their phobia would disappear once the cause had been pinpointed. In some cases, five, ten years had gone by and recovery seemed no nearer, though they had learned some interesting facts about themselves. As one member explained, 'My analyst says I'm afraid to go out in case I see a bus. A bus is a phallic symbol you see, and Dr X says my problem is basically a sexual one.' This woman had spent a month in hospital some fifteen years earlier after being knocked down by a bus; her agoraphobia had developed soon afterwards.

If the origins of agoraphobia and less general phobias can be traced to incidents in the past history of the sufferer, this does not mean that cure will automatically follow. What psychotherapy can do is give the patient an understanding of his present reactions in the light of the past, and from there the patient has something concrete to tackle, resulting in an improved life pattern. Ruth Hurst Vose, in her book *Agoraphobia*, admits she felt cleansed by her psychotherapeutic experiences:

> Like many people, I initially regarded psychotherapy with great suspicion and I did not relish the thought of 'lying on a couch talking about sex'. In fact, I did not have to lie on a couch and the therapist rarely told me what he thought but helped me to find out what I really felt, which was a much more hair-raising experience. Psychotherapy helped me to see the emotional origins of my fears and, by a thorough emotional catharsis, get rid of feelings blocked up in the past. It gave me the gift of knowing why I needed agoraphobia to keep me in the house . . .

Aside from psychotherapy, there are a number of other options open to sufferers of agoraphobia, panic attacks and fears. And the list is growing. Panic attacks have become an acceptable 'neurosis' as such. The expression panic attack have found their way into our everyday vocabulary and has been generalized to mean any number of things – covering conditions ranging from mild fright or panic, to feelings verging on a nervous breakdown. Because of this generalization, and although its numerous connotations are not strictly true, more time and energy has been expended – publicly – to find a cure for panic- or anxiety-related disorders. The following are some of the therapies available, both past and present.

# Electro-Convulsive Therapy

One of the reasons why so many agoraphobia sufferers refused to seek treatment in the past was that they knew the condition was frequently treated by ECT (Electro-Convulsive Therapy). Thirty years ago, when it was assumed that agoraphobia was linked with depression, many people underwent shock treatment for something they did not suffer from. And needless to say it did nothing for their phobia. Depressed? Of course they were depressed; they were faced with the possibility of becoming permanently housebound and no one could explain to them what exactly was the matter. In the majority of cases the depression was caused by the agoraphobia, not vice versa.

These days, ECT has no place in the treatment of primary phobias but is still used in cases of severe depressive illnesses in which there can occasionally be phobic symptoms. In these cases the electrical treatment is directed to depression and not to the phobic symptoms themselves.

Until around the nineteen-fifties people with phobias and anxiety states received little help. It was all right if you were very well off and could afford expensive analysis. And your friends and relatives probably accepted that you were a hypersensitive soul and treated you accordingly.

For ordinary mortals, treatment in psychiatric hospitals and therapy such as drugs – bromides, barbiturates, etc. – and ECT were the norm, accompanied by the stigma of being a 'mental' patient. No wonder sufferers kept quiet about their problems. It is not surprising that there appear to be so many more people with phobias and anxiety states these days. Improvements in treatments available and their publicity through the media has at least given them some hope. The phobia support organizations don't hear quite so often the thankful cry, 'I thought I was the only person in the world who suffered this way.'

When I was going through my worst agoraphobia period in my early twenties I decided that I would see a psychiatrist and find out if any treatment was available. 'Any of the therapies available today might result in your symptoms getting worse,' he told me. 'Recovery is in your own hands.' I paid his hefty fee and wobbled down Harley Street in my usual agitated way, reassured that I was *not* seriously mentally ill and determined to get over the problem on my own. That was in 1952.

## Behaviour Therapy

Behaviour therapy became the most popular treatment for phobias in the sixties. Behaviourists believe that because a phobia can be 'learned', the sufferer can be treated by changing his or her behaviour patterns. Their opinion is that the phobic patient has learned to react wrongly to certain stimuli so must be retrained correctly and without fear.

Professor Isaac Marks of the Institute of Psychiatry in London and leader of the behaviourist school in this country says:

> Behavioural treatment does not assume that phobias are symbolic transformations of hidden difficulties . . . instead, it regards the phobia or obsession itself as the main handicap and tries to eliminate it directly, not by trying to uncover unconscious meanings, but by teaching the sufferer how to face those situations which trigger his discomfort so that he can eventually come to tolerate them . . . Effective behavioural techniques known under various names have in common the principle of exposure to that which frightens you until you get used to it.

The technique which the behavioural therapists still consider to be the most effective and quickest way to overcome phobias is known as *flooding*, which is a pretty good description since it is comparable with being pushed into the deep end of a swimming pool when you cannot swim. You (probably) learn to swim quite quickly, but it is not a pleasant experience!

The theory is that the patient is exposed to her most dreaded situation and encouraged to remain within it, experiencing the most unpleasant sensations that her phobia can produce, facing the panic and distress until the peak is past and the terrifying symptoms gradually evaporate. This might take a few minutes, or it might take an hour or two, but the important point is that the sufferer stands her ground until the anxiety starts to lessen, and has to be prepared to remain until it does.

The phobic patient's greatest dread is that her system can not tolerate the acute phase of a panic attack; that there must be some terrible climax which will prove fatal. This is not so; when the panic feelings reach a peak there is only one way they can go – down. They will gradually subside and the sufferer will find herself sick and shaky but still in one piece . . . and a step nearer recovery.

There is no doubt that such an experience is more exhausting than exhilarating, but it cannot be denied that *if the patient is well prepared by her therapist and has the motivation and the*

36

*courage to cooperate, this can be one of the fastest ways to overcome phobias.*

Even if this type of therapy were readily available throughout the country, the majority of those needing treatment could not take advantage of it. Tense and hypersensitive, in a state of chronic anxiety, for them the prospect of the flooding ordeal would be out of the question. The very thought of participating in treatment of any kind can be distressing to someone whose over-active imagination causes her to anticipate and experience the unpleasant symptoms that strike in her phobic situations.

'I try so hard to fight it,' sufferers say, as though they were about to go into battle. *Fight?* You can just imagine them clenching their fists, gritting their teeth, breathing fast and building up so much nervous energy in their determination to overcome any feelings of panic that the tension becomes unbearable and their brave resolutions are defeated. Anticipating fear in the mind is equivalent to experiencing fear in reality, and the average phobia sufferer – with the over-active imagination which is frequently part of the phobic personality – is permanently exposed to dreaded situations, living in them day and night. Is this not a type of flooding? If flooding is meant to help, why has she not been able to cure herself long ago?

'Once we confront our fear determinedly it will diminish,' writes Professor Marks. 'If we do not understand the fear we cannot confront it, we continually run away from it and not having the knowledge to tackle it positively we are overwhelmed.'

**Systematic Desensitization:** This form of behaviour therapy is more popular with patients than therapists, basically because it is more comfortable. It takes much longer to work up to the difficult part and since the therapists want to get on with the job they are inclined to favour a more forceful approach.

Where self help is concerned, this is an ideal way to start, as we shall see in Chapter 14.

The first part of the treatment concentrates on helping the patient to achieve a state of complete relaxation, and this is no easy feat where phobic people are concerned. For a start, the effort of making the journey to the hospital or day centre often results in the patient arriving in a state of nervous exhaustion, with the prospect of the return trip home after treatment another ordeal to be faced.

Tense and nervous people have forgotten how to relax and have to be taught this skill through exercise and deep breathing techniques. The phobic person finds this very difficult; the idea of 'letting go' is frightening when your whole life is concentrated on trying to control your emotions. To lie on a couch and to submit to another person's instructions may actually increase the tension. It is the old story of feeling trapped; instinct tells you to open your eyes, sit up, put your feet on the floor and get out quick!

Perseverance and a sympathetic therapist will gradually over-come the patient's aversion and then the next stage can be tackled. As we have seen, a vivid imagination can cause an immense amount of distress and it is important to channel that imagination in the right direction. From constantly visualizing phobic situations and experiencing the accompanying physical symptoms and mental distress, the patient is encouraged to imagine places and situations in which she would feel comfort-able, the therapist encouraging her to experience feelings of peace and tranquillity. Sometimes music or tapes of familiar loved sounds or voices may be played in the background. If one can learn the techniques of relaxation, create an imaginary haven to drift into instead of the nightmare of out-of-control negative thoughts and fantasies, the first step to recovery has been taken.

When the outside world is a threatening place it can be attractive, once she has acquired the knack, for an agoraphobe or someone with a distressing phobia to retreat more and more into a fantasy life where anxieties disappear. This is particularly evident with children and adolescents and can lead to permanent withdrawal if not controlled. The next step for the therapist is to make the imagination work towards a positive goal, and persuade the patient to imagine a mildly unpleasant situation, at the same time consciously holding on to the feelings of calm that her happier mind pictures produce. Once she can face this situation with the minimum of distress, she will be encouraged to tackle a more difficult one, gradually progressing through her dreaded places until she can visualize herself coping with the situation she feels it would be impossible to face in real life.

Desensitization in fantasy is a long drawn-out procedure and when possible, treatment is speeded up by persuading the patient to tackle the initial step – the mildly upsetting situation – first in imagination and then in reality. Between treatment sessions she must practise facing the problems every day, remaining relaxed and calm as she has been taught. When she is ready she will take the next step, and from there will gradually progress through her list of black spots until she reaches her goal – the place she dreads the most.

Back in the early years of the Open Door, agoraphobic members wrote enthusiastically in the newsletter about their experiences with desensitization therapy. For many of them this seemed to be the answer, though it was frustrating for those who had no treatment facilities in their particular area. Success stories were circulated as patients gingerly emerged through their front doors, walked to the next house, to the corner of the street, to the shops. It looked as though many of them were on the way to recovery:

'I haven't had a panic for weeks . . .'
'I can face the supermarket without dreading a return of the old feelings.'
'Sat right through the church service feeling great.'

But the euphoria did not last and sooner or later the majority of the desensitization patients started backsliding. What was wrong? They had thought that by learning to relax and remaining calm they could avoid panics and that their previous unpleasant symptoms had gone for good. Unfortunately, sooner or later they found that this was not the case; moving around freely, anxiety gradually faded to mild apprehension and confidence was returning when out of the blue the old panic struck once more and the patient found herself distressed, disappointed and determined not to venture out again. All the efforts to get back to normal had ended in failure. Agoraphobia and/or fear was still there.

Sadly, many of these people refused to try again; they could not accept the fact that it is a necessary part of recovery to experience the panics and all the accompanying symptoms, in order to learn how to cope with them and eventually overcome them. Nowadays, patients are left in little doubt before they start treatment that they must learn to face their fears, and the outcome of their efforts is considerably more successful.

Another behaviour therapy technique involved patients being taken out individually or in groups, by therapists who were able to give the necessary support and encouragement to those trying to cope with anxiety and panic and lead them through a series of difficult situations. They went to busy town centres, travelled on buses and trains, queued in shops and pushed through crowds. These exercises proved helpful in that the patients were given the chance to experience phobic problems with professional support. But the agoraphobe is an odd bird. Some feel bad in any and every situation, but others have very definite trouble spots peculiar to themselves. It is difficult to explain why one side of a road feels hostile and the other 'safe'. Passing a certain building, a particular tree, a church with a tall spire, can cause anxiety to build up. Even the lighting in a famous chain of shops can for some reason be an anxiety-provoking factor. A person who is mildly agoraphobic, perhaps without even realizing it, may unconsciously plot a route to avoid 'hostile' spots and steer an erratic course between her home and her destination, crossing to one side of the road at one point, then back again further on.

In their normal everyday lives there was no reason for some of these patients to travel on tube trains or rush around city centres. In therapy they were learning to cope with such situations, but so often their problem lay much nearer home – the place where the phobic habit had been established.

The phobic personality is afraid of the physical feelings she experiences in certain situations and she must be taught to cope with these feelings – *not the situation*. Otherwise, even though she learns to deal with a number of her dreaded spots, she will be likely to panic when in a new one.

*Graduated Exposure:* Very simply, the phobic patient is told to make a list of her fears, grading them from mild to unbearably terrifying. With the therapist she tackles them one at a time, becoming tolerant of each minor fear before proceeding to the next one in the hierarchy.

For monosymptomatic or single phobias this works very well but for the agoraphobic or social phobic person who is expected to present herself at the hospital for treatment this initial effort is really a form of flooding which many sufferers *cannot* tolerate at this stage.

How can we estimate how many phobic patients are benefiting from treatment when the most severely affected cannot get to the hospital? Patients who are accepted for therapy are those who are within easy reach of a hospital and can be helped to make the initial journey. There must also be a high degree of motivation in a patient confident and determined enough to persevere with treatment.

Ideally, the therapist should visit the patient at home and take her through the first phase of treatment until she has reached the stage where she can *get* to the hospital. This, of course, is wishful thinking. There are just not enough therapists to treat patients in hospital, never mind the hundreds who would be needed to go into the homes of those who need them so badly.

Here I am not talking necessarily of totally housebound sufferers – there are fewer of these than the media would lead us to believe – but those who are operating fairly normally on the surface though within a limited area. In the absence of any trained therapist the sufferer is forced to rely on her own self-help programme and any member of her family, close friend or fellow sufferer from a self-help group if available. But what about the family doctor?

# General Practitioners

In an ideal situation, the understanding GP will explain the condition, removing fears of insanity and ominous physical diseases and giving sensible advice and treatment. In so many cases, unfortunately, the doctor himself does not understand what he or she may consider irrational panic or fear, and can add to the patient's distress by adopting the all-too-familiar 'snap-out-of-it' attitude. Too often the problem has to do with lack of communication when the doctor has little time to deal with a patient who seems incapable of explaining her problem coherently. One single woman sufferer noted:

> My GP is a kind but bluff fatherly type who has little time for 'nervy' women. He talks *at* me but won't give me a chance to explain, so I come away from the surgery feeling I have got nowhere. I try to tell him about my nerves and he launches into a three-minute lecture supposed to be reassuring but which just makes me feel guilty about making a fuss.

'I cannot discuss anything with my doctor' is a typical protest. 'There is never the time to explain, and if I *have* managed to make the journey to his surgery and had to sit in the waiting room, I am in such a state that I can't remember half the things I wanted to say' is another common complaint.

In these days, very few doctors will make a house call except in a case of emergency, and it is terribly difficult for an agora-phobic or frightened person not only to face the ordeal of a visit to the surgery, but to be able to discuss the condition coherently when they get there. In years gone by, patients looked upon their family doctor as a friend and counsellor, but doctors now have little time to live up to that image. Worse still, a good many are downright unsympathetic to those whom they consider to be neurotic and have little inclination to go into the problem in any depth.

Oh, but in recent years their attitude has changed you may say. Has it?

In the spring of 1991, a woman I'll call Jackie phoned me in tears. Her doctor – a woman – had told her she is thoroughly selfish and has only herself to blame for her agoraphobia. 'She shouted at me and banged on the table,' said Jackie. 'Then she increased my Valium from one a day [size of dosage not specified] to four a day and gave me a prescription for 200.' Jackie's former doctor had prescribed small amounts as Jackie has a history of suicide attempts.

Chris asked her GP if she could cut down on her tranquillizers as she wished to come off them altogether. 'He tore up the prescription he had just written, threw the pieces on the floor and told me to find another doctor.'

Madeleine said, 'When I finished trying to explain to my doctor he just looked at me and yawned.'

Of course there are thousands of dedicated, caring doctors who go out of their way to visit anxious patients in their homes and go to considerable lengths to find where specialist help may be available, but more often than not, five minute appointments and queues at surgeries preclude anything other than a cursory check-up, and an oft unneeded prescription for depressants, anti-depressants or pain-killers.

Sadly, therapy just is not available in many parts of the country and in other areas there is often a waiting list of anything up to two years. Many treatment centres and hospital departments treating phobias and anxiety states have had to close down because of the present economic situation, though one hopes the situation will improve in the future.

## FLOATING THROUGH FEAR

In the sixties an Australian physician arrived on the scene with a message that brought hope and relief to everyone who suffered from anxiety, panic attacks, phobias and every kind of nervous disorder. Dr Claire Weekes' book *Self Help for Your Nerves* became the most requested book in Britain's public libraries together with her subsequent books which all carry the same message – that those who had nervous problems were not suffering from some dire mental disorder but from an over sensitized nervous system. Fear of the fear is what dominates so many people's lives and Dr Weekes tells her readers that they must face up to their fear, to *accept* fear and not to fight against it. By accepting fear you learn to 'float through it', so that you relax instead of increasing stress by trying to fight it.

Dr Weekes was probably best known for her work in the study and treatment of agoraphobia. Her books, records, tapes and her radio and television appearances have carried her message to sufferers throughout the world. Many contemporary psychiatrists and doctors practise her techniques.

Many members of the Open Door were helped by Claire Weekes. One wrote:

> I know I still have a long way to go but I have made so much progress and have a real sense of achievement knowing that I have done it all on my own. I take Dr Weekes' advice and float through the odd panic which still knocks me about once a week. The important thing is that I am not afraid of the panics any more – understanding the fear of fear and knowing how to cope with it makes all the difference. Also, instead of fretting about what might have been and what might be in store in the future, I take one day at a time, looking forwards to the day when I know I shall be free of this wretched complaint.

Psychotherapy does help some sufferers, but there are alternative forms of treatment you can try.

# 3
# IT'S NOT ALWAYS IN THE MIND

## A PHYSIOLOGICAL CAUSE?

An American psychiatrist recently suggested that ninety per cent of phobias are due to an easily diagnosable inner-ear dysfunction and *not* to emotional illness. He noted that most inner-ear-based phobias respond favourably to a series of anti-motion-sickness and related medications and that most panic episodes are related to a similar underlying physical disorder.

Dr Harold Levinson is a member of the American Medical and Psychiatric Association and is Clinical Associate Professor of Psychiatry at New York University Medical Center. In his book *Phobia Free*, Dr Levinson explains and diagnoses the physical components of phobic behaviour, showing us that a fear of travelling, for example, may be the result of an inner-ear failure to handle motion input – resulting in a panic attack. A fear of getting lost or going far from home could be explained as a simple directional dysfunction within the inner-ear system. A fear of heights might result from a sense of imbalance.

An integral part of our anxiety-control network is located in the cerebellar-vestibular system, the 'inner-ear' system. If this system is weakened the entire anxiety-control network may be affected and the body may not be able to regulate anxiety so that even a moderate amount of anxiety can escalate into acute fear and panic.

One of the functions of the inner-ear system is to act as a gyroscope controlling balance. If this balance system is impaired it can be further unsettled by heights, lifts, open spaces and many other situations. When you are unbalanced and dizzy you experience anxiety. Sense of direction can also be affected, you can become hypersensitive to motion, which may cause different kinds of travel phobia. Bright, flickering lights, even certain colours or patterns can trigger anxiety as the inner-ear system processes all visual information. In the same way, because all sound information is filtered, sequenced and tuned by the inner-ear system, impairment may cause hypersensitivity to loud or piercing noises.

Causes of inner-ear dysfunction can be due to severe or repeated ear or sinus infections, glandular fever, concussion or a number of other disorders. Also, fluctuating hormone levels — often due to pregnancy, menstruation or the menopause — may be a cause. As many people have discovered, drugs, or withdrawal from drugs can also cause acute anxiety and phobias, particularly agoraphobia, which may also be due to inner-ear dysfunction.

## The Cures

Medications which specifically target the inner-ear system include a variety of anti-motion-sickness drugs, antihistamines, vitamins, and stimulants known to improve vestibular functioning. These medications often result in rapid and dramatic improvements in phobic behaviour and related anxiety symptoms.

Medication may well improve any problems in the inner-ear system but remember that the psychologically triggered anticipatory anxiety may well remain and will have to be treated by other methods, such as graduated exposure to the phobic situation or objects which are causing distress.

When I wrote about Dr Levinson's book in the PAX newsletter I received one of the biggest reactions ever from members who felt that many of their balance and dizziness problems had led to acute anxiety and panic attacks because they had no idea what was happening to them.

Mary wrote:

Thank goodness the medical profession is at last admitting that there are sometimes physical causes for some phobias instead of trying to persuade us that 'it's all in the mind'. I have had trouble with dizzy spells for years and am fed up with being told I'm neurotic and should stay on tranquillizers.

Grace wrote:

My mother suffered from Meniere's Disease for many years and this caused her to become housebound. It seemed to be acceptable forty years ago and no one thought her neurotic or 'odd'. Now I have constant dizziness which prevents me from doing many things, but this is diagnosed as part of a general anxiety state and I am made to feel something of a second-class citizen.

As for me, my worst agoraphobic period started after I had recovered from a bout of flu. Waiting at a bus stop I turned my head sharply to the right and the resulting giddiness culminated in the worst panic attack I had experienced since childhood . . . and seven years of agoraphobia, anticipatory anxiety and panic attacks ensued.

I recovered from my anxiety problems – but I still can not turn my head sharply to the right without feeling dizzy, even if I am lying in bed. The important thing is that I am not frightened by the sensation. I wish I had read Dr Levinson's book when I was young.

# NEURO-DEVELOPMENTAL DELAY

Did you crawl when you were a young child? Perhaps you took your first tottering steps at an early age, to the delight of your parents who felt you were more advanced than the creeping, grubby-kneed babies of their friends. Do you kick a ball with your right foot, but catch it in your left hand? These questions may appear to have little to do with panic and phobias, but psychologist Peter Blythe at the Institute for Neuro-Physiological Psychology in Chester, has discovered that many phobic sufferers have definite physical characteristics which could, under certain conditions, be a cause of anxiety and panic attacks.

We are all born with a number of infant survival reflexes which are controlled by the brain during the first months of life, after which time they are gradually replaced by appropriate adult reflexes. The babies of our primitive ancestors had to cling tightly as their mother swung through the trees or fled from danger – a reflex that was vital for their survival. Today's newborn will still grip firmly to a proffered finger and hang on tightly while being lifted.

Babies can swim when only a few weeks old. If placed in the water in a prone position, they do not struggle but make reflex swimming movements which actually propel them forward. However, by the time they are four months old, they have lost this automatic swimming response; they rotate into a supine position, struggle and clutch at adult hands for support.

Thousands of years ago, these and other reflexes were necessary if the baby was to survive and they still exist in each child today until such time as they are no longer necessary. Some of us, for one reason or another, retain as adults certain infant survival reflexes which should have been controlled by the brain before we were two years old.

Sometimes a difficult birth, a feverish illness such as measles or whooping cough can result in a weakened central nervous system caused by brain dysfunction. Many children are affected in this way and it should not be confused with brain damage, but seen rather as a difficulty in controlling functions.

Peter Blythe originally referred to this condition as OBD – Organic Brain Dysfunction – but because doctors in the USA used this term to describe a type of psychosis caused by damage to the brain, Blythes's definition is now known as NDD, Neuro-Developmental Delay. He believes it is caused by adult reflexes not developing to take the place of infant reflexes.

Brain dysfunction . . . a weakened central nervous system – diagnoses which will give a real nervous jolt to many readers of this book, but fear not! NDD is not some terrible disability which is going to cripple you; in fact, the majority of those with NDD are not affected by it at all, since their brains will compensate. In some cases, however, the brain compensation will be too much to cope with and the person will be prone to anxiety and other problems.

In her book *Agoraphobia*, Ruth Hurst Vose, writes:

Put very simply, if the reflexes of childhood are not transformed into adult reflexes which are necessary for our proper functions as an adult, we are going to be in trouble both emotionally and physically. It has been found that if more than two primitive reflexes are still with us as adults we are much more prone to stress and the disorders this brings.

It is a relief to know that not only can NDD be detected but the amount of dysfunction can be measured and, most important, corrected.

In the early years of this century, Sigmund Freud said he believed that one day someone would find a physical basis for neurosis. Recently, Professor Isaac Marks wrote: 'We are left with the question of the origin of the general anxiety in agoraphobics. No one has yet answered this adequately.'

There is mounting evidence to show that there is definitely a physical basis for panic attacks. Isaac Marks notes that, 'There is a sub-group of agoraphobes whose eyes play tricks and cause a type of panic attack,' while Dr Claire Weekes wrote: '. . . In my opinion to put agoraphobia in the first place and general anxiety in the second is to reverse their true order. The majority of my patients first developed an anxiety state from which agoraphobia arose as a secondary phase.'

It is accepted that all anxiety states are accompanied by some degree of physical sensation and discomfort caused by an upset of the nervous system. The anxiety triggers off a stress reaction in the body, causing the unpleasant symptoms the phobic sufferer recognizes only too well. This has resulted in many doctors telling patients that all their experienced symptoms are the result of their anxiety state.

ANXIETY CAN CAUSE UNPLEASANT PHYSICAL SYMPTOMS.
UNPLEASANT PHYSICAL SYMPTOMS CAN CAUSE ANXIETY.

Which comes first?

Blythe defines two different types of agoraphobia. The first is the psychological type, where there is a definite phobic fear that something terrible is going to happen – a calamity syndrome. These purely emotional agoraphobia sufferers form about twenty-five to thirty per cent of the agoraphobic population; generally speaking, since their condition is due to emotional factors and learned behaviour when the patient is frightened to go out, it will respond to whichever therapy they find most helpful.

The remaining seventy to seventy-five per cent of agoraphobic and anxiety sufferers have some degree of NDD, which makes them prone to stress symptoms. When under pressure, they find that their eyes play tricks and their balancing mechanism is upset, making them feel dizzy and unsafe. Their continued effort to keep control increases the internal stress level, resulting in emotional distress.

A link between a dysfunction in the balancing mechanism and resulting anxiety was made by Feldenkrais (1949) when he described dizziness as being connected with a disorder of the balancing mechanism, which frightened the sufferer and caused pallor, nausea, vomiting and breathing and pulse alterations.

In a paper by Woolfson, Marlowe, Silverstein and Keels (1981), the authors made a statement which is relevant to panic sufferers: 'Patients are often emotionally upset after an episode of vertigo and especially when it develops without warning, they may become extremely frightened . . .'

The important point about this statement is that most sufferers complain of either objective vertigo – when the person feels as if she is stationary and the objects seem to move around her – or subjective vertigo, when she feels as if she is turning in a stationary environment. Because the majority experience their first attack of vertigo without any warning whatsoever, they quickly develop a 'neurotic' fear of it happening again.

Peter Blythe explains that man is a biped animal, dependent upon his balancing mechanism to keep his upright position in space:

If he suffers from 'gravitational insecurity' because his balancing

50

mechanism is not functioning properly, the lack of balance and resulting feeling of insecurity gives rise to anxiety; stress hormones are released, causing even greater internal excitation and anxiety . . .

Sufferers with NDD problems are generally found to be 'stimulus bound', which means they are unable to ignore irrelevant movements going on around them. Disturbed by too much action and too many people moving in their field of vision, and becoming overwhelmed by a barrage of stimuli, they feel that they are going to fall over or faint. Most sufferers will describe these sensations and we begin to see why 'fear of the market place' is not such a bad description of the more severe problem of agoraphobia. The agoraphobic sufferers who prefer to go out after dark or who feel 'safer' when wearing dark glasses are subconsciously trying to cut down on the disturbing stimulus of sound and noise that is going on around them. 'Where there is a concentration of irregular movement, noise and bright light,' says Ruth Hurst Vose, 'the stimulus can get too much and the central nervous system will "blow a fuse".' Some years ago, an Open Door member described an outing with a nurse-therapist and four other patients. Her agoraphobia had improved and she had not experienced a panic attack for several months. On this occasion it was decided that the group would make a journey on the Underground:

The prospect of plunging into the bowels of the earth did not bother me, strangely enough. I coped with the escalator, though the movement had always upset me before as I felt so unsafe and wobbly. The lighting was a slight problem and the others in the group laughed at me when I put my dark glasses on. It was when I heard the train coming that I knew I was in for trouble, but I gritted my teeth and got in. The doors closed and then as the train started the awful noise began to build up. The movement and the sound made my head spin and I thought my ears would burst; I tried to keep myself under control as I didn't want to upset the others, who I knew might react badly, but I had the sort of acute panic I had not experienced for months and when we got out at the next stop I had to sit on a seat on the platform and gasp for breath. I knew I was over-breathing which made things worse and the sound of another train approaching was the final straw. I fled for the escalator and kept going until I got outside into the open air. I was afraid this was going to be a real setback, but once I had realized that never never again would there be any necessity for me to go on the tube I felt happier and continued to make progress.

Another member suffered from what everyone, himself included, considered a 'dental phobia'. He found it difficult to understand, as he had never had any traumatic experiences while undergoing dental treatment, but suddenly realized that it was the chair which was the problem. As soon as he was tilted backwards he felt insecure and dizzy, with the usual anxiety feelings building up. With the help of an interested and understanding dentist he gradually overcame the anxiety, receiving treatment while sitting upright on a dining-room chair, then gradually accustoming himself to tolerating the angle of the surgery chair.

Another person with balancing and perceptual problems was a twelve-year old boy whose mother wrote:

Neil had been having problems with school phobia and we had reached the stage where he was refusing to go to school at all. The school doctor was very helpful and after much questioning decided that the problem lay in PE lessons . . . Neil has always been rather uncoordinated, but he denied that there was any teasing from other boys about his clumsiness. We found that his real dread was having to do handstands, 'forward rolls' and hanging upside-down from the wall bars. We realized that much of his problem might have a physical foundation, though a full medical examination showed that he was in good health and his eyesight normal. The PE instructor and school doctor between them devised a sort of remedial programme and twice a week Neil has special lessons on his own in which he is taught gradually to do certain exercises until he can cope with the feelings of disorientation associated with being upside-down. He now only participates in the class exercises when he wants to – the explanation to the other boys is that he has ear problems. The change in him is remarkable . . . it is frightening to realize that such a relatively minor problem can have such a drastic effect on a child's wellbeing . . .

Each person in the above examples may well have had NDD problems with which they were able unconsciously to come to terms. It seems significant that discovering the cause of their anxiety helped them to overcome their fears of specific situations.

People with brain dysfunction may have problems with spatial orientation – experiencing difficulties in distinguishing left from right and having no sense of direction when they attempt to read a map or to navigate whilst driving (Bellak, 1979):

> Failure to establish clear boundaries in turn has an effect on object relations, leading to insufficient individualization and a poorly defined self-image. Typically both children and adults with minimal brain dysfunction feel perplexed, and others suffer from the uncomfortable sensation of being lost, which may at times produce high levels of anxiety.

The Institute for Neuro-Physiological Psychology in Chester will carry out extensive tests for dysfunction in a patient and can also measure the percentage of dysfunction, correcting it with a programme of simple remedial exercises tailored to the individual. The patient is also screened to establish that the problems are due to basic organic faults and not purely emotional.

If the emotional screening shows that the suffering has a psychological foundation, the appropriate therapy can be worked out by the Institute.

Certain apparently unrelated questions do help to pinpoint which part of the nervous system is weakened. See if any of these might apply in your case.

1. Did you have problems at school while in the gym?
2. Did you suffer from travel sickness as a child?
3. During school assembly, did you occasionally have the fear that you would faint or fall over?
4. When you are very tired, do you lose coordination and become clumsy? Do you drop things, miss the door handle, etc?
5. Do you become anxious if there are too many people

moving about around you, or if too many people talk at the same time?

~ 6. When very tired, do you find that you know what you want to say, but what you actually say is not what you intend?

~ 7. Do you have difficulty in differentiating between left and right?

The Institute has found that if the sufferer who has lost the ability to compensate for underlying organic brain dysfunction is put on to a remedial programme of exercises – and does them regularly in their own home – the prospect of success is very good.

In her book, Ruth Hurst Vose describes how agoraphobia wrecked her professional and private life until after two and a half years of psychoanalysis and hypnotherapy she had improved 'beyond all hope'; she then decided to try to speed up her recovery by undergoing a series of tests at the Institute, to see if there were any physical, neurological or emotional impediments to her recovery which were as yet undetected:

> Not only had the personality tests revealed my character precisely and most uncomfortably . . . but there was also neurological evidence of minimal or organic brain dysfunction – difficulties of functioning caused by small faults within the central nervous system. My gross muscle coordination was not very good, and I had such problems with eye muscle movement that to focus my eyes on an object cost me a great deal more effort than for people with normal eyes . . .
>
> The effect of the first exercise programme was immediate. I had unconsciously been using my left eye for sighting when doing close work, but on the first day of wearing the eye-patch, which took the stress off my eye muscles and forced me to focus with my right eye, my temper improved dramatically. Within a short time I found I could work for longer periods without getting tired and the feelings of unreality and depersonalization slowly diminished.

Psychotherapy helped Ruth to speed up her recovery as she 'galloped through a series of emotional explosions', clearing the psychological problems which she realized had appeared largely as a result of her brain dysfunctions. Having made a complete recovery, Ruth has been able to resume her professional life as a writer, lecturer and publicity consultant.

Another patient successfully treated by Blythe is John, a high-powered businessman and lecturer who had been suffering from agoraphobia for twenty-five years since adolescence. Within six weeks of starting treatment, the perceptual problems which had caused him to see distorted images had disappeared, other dysfunctions had also been corrected and John was able to fly around the world on a business trip, euphoric with the new feeling of freedom that he was experiencing.

Looking back over forty years to when my anxiety state was affecting my school life, I can see so many indications that I must have had NDD problems. I was and am completely ambidextrous − cross-laterality has been associated with a vulnerability to physical stress. I never crawled − a child who has not developed a transformed tonic neck reflex will never go through the stages of crawling and will have lost out on a vital stage in neural development. Turning my head suddenly to the right or looking upwards made me feel 'odd', while being blindfolded produced feelings of acute disorientation − visual perceptual problems which are to do not with sight, but with how the eye muscles work and the signals the eyes send back to the visual cortex of the brain.

The Institute has found that in thirty to fifty per cent of the sufferers, there appears to be an hereditary factor. My mother, who was also agoraphobic for many years, has exactly the same physical idiosyncrasies as I have; the fact that we each fought our way through agoraphobia to emerge as well-balanced individuals with particularly steady nerves was partly good luck but mostly hard work and a determination to recover. I am personally convinced that Peter Blythe is working in the right direction in finding a cause and cure for the background problems of agoraphobia and anxiety.

Of course, when the physical abnormalities have been corrected there will still be the habits of agoraphobia and panic to deal with but without these background problems, cracking the habit should be much easier.

Within the last three years the *American Journal of Psychiatry* has carried two important papers. One of these revealed that a study had found that sixty-seven percent of agoraphobia and panic disorder patients had vestibular problems. The other paper which appeared more recently showed how panic attacks came from a dysfunction – an error in functioning – within the brain itself, which caused psychological problems.

Peter Blythe is insistent that even when there is a physical basis for agoraphobia and panic disorders, the frightening experiences which the basic physical faults create soon result in the person developing a 'fear of fear' which is indeed neurotic; but that is a secondary neurosis and not a primary one causing the problem.

Patients undergoing NDD therapy are given a series of reflex-inhibition movements which, depending upon what reflexes are found to be incorrect, they do each day for six to fourteen minutes. As they start to get better, the programme may be altered. At the same time many patients on the reflex-inhibition programme do need supportive psychotherapy to deal with the 'fear of fear' which may have developed. Also, they may need some medication during the period in which their system is being corrected. The average time patients are on the programme is a year, and its success rate is very promising.

Pamela was phobic for forty years, her main problem being an inability to eat in front of other people because of a difficulty in swallowing. After twenty years of seeking help unsuccessfully she embarked on a course of NDD therapy.

Not only does the theory make absolute sense to me but the therapy has proved extremely effective. Stress no longer brings me to my knees (literally). I do not have to swallow a handful of Valium every time I do something unfamiliar/exciting/fearful . . . I can now enjoy the sun and the beach and open spaces, and the theatre. I enjoy my food now. Above all, I sleep much better – I do not find myself clinging to the doorpost in the middle of just about every night in absolute terror, fighting for breath and seemingly life itself.

And lastly, but not least, I have re-gained some of the self-respect denied to me for most of my life. I am not one of life's 'neurotics' after all. Peter Blythe has proved that there has been an organic basis to my problems. How many other 'neurotics' out there could, if given the chance, say the same, I wonder – the majority I suspect.

It will be interesting to see how this form of treatment develops, and, hopefully, many more people will be helped through this approach.

# 4

# THE TROUBLE WITH TRANQUILLIZERS

There are many people who are waiting hopefully for the magic pill that will banish all their fears and unpleasant symptoms of anxiety. When tranquillizers first arrived on the scene in the sixties they were hailed as a boon and a blessing, the answer to every anxiety sufferer's prayer. There were few homes in the country where a bottle of 'happy' pills was not in the medicine cupboard.

The advantage of these new drugs, we were told, was that they were safe and non-addictive and soon everyone, patients and doctors alike, began to regard tranquillizers as the answer to every problem caused by stress, anxiety and emotional upsets. They were a boon for over-worked doctors who could rarely spare the time needed to counsel patients but were thankful to prescribe indefinitely for those who felt the need to continue with their tranquillizers.

Unfortunately nervous patients began to regard the tranquillizers as a crutch to help them limp through life. It was hardly surprising that problems began to arise, and those who had been taking the drugs over a long period found themselves dependent on them. Once the beneficial effects wore off they were faced with having to cope with a different set of symptoms *as well as* the situation which had led to them taking tranquillizers in the first place.

When life becomes painful because of sickness or bereavement, divorce, or the serious illness of one's partner, parents or children, tranquillizers are often prescribed to help the patient weather the acute stages of the situation and are accepted thankfully. The pain is dulled for the present and facing the realities of the situation can be put aside for the time being. Yes, tranquillizers do deaden the pain but they also deaden one's ability to face up to the situation and deal with it.

Tranquillizers are used as a muscle relaxant, as an anti-convulsant to treat various forms of epilepsy, and after many severe illnesses or major surgery when the patient needs to slow down — after heart operations for instance. But sometimes, even in these cases, there are unfortunate consequences:

> After my hysterectomy I was prescribed tranquillizers to keep me calm and help me to cope with my three young children. But I found I was even less able to manage because my mind was so dull and I became very distressed because of my inability to handle the kids.
> Luckily, my GP was very understanding and agreed that the pills were doing me more harm than good. Practical help with the children was more important and my mother moved in for a month. Once my mind felt normal I felt generally better.

One man in his fifties wrote:

> I never thought of myself as a nervous person but after heart surgery I was prescribed tranquillizers. At first I protested, then I began to think I couldn't cope without them as I was experiencing flashes of anxiety — a sensation new to me. I found myself telling my GP that I didn't feel ready to come off them, I would wait just a little longer. My heart was fine, now the problem appeared to be my nerves! It has taken me a long time to be free of the effects of the drugs and to feel a normal person once more.

## How the Problem Arose. . .

Tranquillizers were widely prescribed for phobias and though they have been ineffective for agoraphobia on the whole, they do appear to help simple and social phobias by lowering anticipatory anxiety and giving the chemical courage required to confront a feared object or situation. Even when they don't work, patients are often loathe to give them up, not because they feel much better when taking them, but because they are afraid of feeling worse if they don't.

People who have been on tranquillizers for any length of time can become lethargic and slow; they may complain of general malaise, and experience aches, pains, stomach upsets and, worst of all, feelings of increasing anxiety and sudden panic attacks. So instead of solving the anxiety problems, tranquillizers may well be at the root. Tranquillizers prescribed for another condition altogether have regularly led to dangerous anxiety-related illnesses, as we can see from this case.

My GP originally prescribed tranquillizers when I was nursing my terminally ill mother and suffering from back problems myself. I was never a nervous person, in fact I was considered the strong one of the family, always able to cope in times of trouble. I continued to take the pills after my mother's death and soon after experienced sudden anxiety attacks when I felt as though something terrible was about to happen. I felt dizzy, had palpitations and thought I was about to faint. Each time it happened I got more and more panicky, telephoning my GP and begging him to come and see me as I was finding it increasingly difficult to leave the house in case I had one of these attacks.

I now realize that I am suffering from classic agoraphobia symptoms and though I am being weaned off the tranquillizers – which I'm sure were the cause of my present problems – I feel I have a long way to go before I feel as I did in the pre-tranquillizer days. Of course my GP and the psychologist he referred me to feel that my anxiety and panic attacks stem from the time of my mother's death. I do not agree.

It is understandable that those suffering from chronic anxiety will look around for something that will help them. When I was agoraphobic I would have been one of the first to ask for tranquillizers, but I missed them by about three years. I was well on the way to recovery when the first to be available came on to the market – and with no prescription needed. It was called Oblivon. Although at the time I was so much better, I still had a horror of dentists and bought a pack of Oblivon when I had a dental appointment. I certainly felt fine during the treatment but I never took another capsule, though I carried them around with me for a couple of years . . . just in case.

## False Security . . . Not a Cure

Doctors do not claim that tranquillizers 'cure' anxiety. The idea is simply that if a person gets so anxious that they cannot cope with life – that their 'functioning' is interfered with – then the drugs will help them to calm down enough to begin to cope again. At some point it is hoped that the patient will stop needing the drugs. Occasionally, tranquillizers may help the user to feel strong enough to tackle the cause of the problem itself.

It is more likely, though, that in a false state of tranquillity the patient will avoid thinking about the real problem and how she is going to do something about it.

Kate suffered from social phobias, fear of meeting people, of eating in public, of travelling on public transport and of the need to dash to the nearest lavatory without warning.

I found that I was almost euphoric when I first started to take tranquillizers. I thought they were going to solve all my problems and I told myself that when they took effect I would be able to get back into life once more. I did feel calmer and less desperate about the situation. Then I had a new doctor – a woman who told me it was time for me to stop relying on the drugs.

Had I been on a bus lately? she asked. Had I in fact tried to face up to *any* of the things I was afraid of or was I still trying to avoid them? She decided it was time I had some psychiatric help and referred me to the local hospital. Now they and I are putting in some constructive work. It's not very agreeable but at least I feel I am getting somewhere at last and though I am still on a low dose of tranquillizers I know that *I* am helping myself.

The organization RELEASE (see page 202 for details) warns that taking a pill for a problem can often make people feel that the problem is that something is wrong with *them*, not what is happening in their life. Because they are anxious and upset they are treated as if they are sick and given medicine. Many people then come to feel that if they were well they *would* be able to cope, that they *should* be able to cope and that the problem must be that they are in some way inadequate. This results in a loss of confidence about themselves.

I know that many of you who are struggling with the 'fear of the fear' might find some of this depressing. I know you are going to skip some of these pages. Remember that knowledge and understanding are important to help you to overcome the problem so don't adopt an ostrich-like attitude hoping that everything will improve without you making an effort. Keep reading!

Taking tranquillizers for a short time during a crisis can be helpful; the danger comes when they are relied on for years and years.

In 1980, the Committee on the Review of Medicines published a report warning that there was no proof of the effectiveness of tranquillizers after four months. This meant that patients who had been taking them for longer had been doing so unnecessarily; the drugs had been doing them no further good. Figures showed that as many as one in six people on a normal dose of tranquillizers will become addicted after taking them for six months, and one in three will get addicted after taking tranquillizers for a year.

When their efficacy wears off the patient will experience all the symptoms that the drug was taken to combat in the first place. Look at John, for example, a freelance journalist in his thirties:

My problem was free-floating anxiety and that was what my doctor prescribed for. At first the drugs helped but latterly I began to have acute panic attacks – something I had not experienced before. I was afraid to go out in case I had a panic attack and eventually became housebound. I had become severely agoraphobic – something I thought happened only to women. My GP keeps prescribing different drugs but I want to come off them altogether and extricate myself from this Catch-22 situation.

## Dependent?

Professor Malcolm Lader at the Maudsley Hospital in London estimates that there may be one hundred thousand people in the UK who are dependent upon tranquillizers. How do you know if you are dependent? If you feel that your pills have stopped working and you have to increase the dose to get the same effect? Or do you feel ill when you do not take the pills? If the answer is yes to either of these then you could be dependent.

If you have been on tranquillizers for a long time you may well experience many of the symptoms for which you originally took the drugs – anxiety, panic attacks, agoraphobia, depression – and you may well feel thoroughly run down, suffering various aches, pains and digestive upsets. Realizing that it may be the tranquillizers themselves that are causing these symptoms will be a step towards recovery. Because you have something specific to worry about – i.e., the effect of tranquillizers upon your system – means that *you* can do something about it, even if the first step to recovery is very small and very painful.

THE VERY FIRST STEP OF ALL IS TO SEE YOUR DOCTOR AND TELL HIM OR HER THAT YOU WISH TO COME OFF YOUR TRANQUILLIZERS. ASK FOR HELP TO ENABLE YOU TO DO THIS.

Information and advice, including telephone counselling is available from CITA – the Council for Involuntary Tranquillizer Addiction – as well as from RELEASE. Telephone numbers and addresses for these and other support groups are at the end of the book.

Some people may cut down and come off their tranquillizers without any side effects at all; others find it more difficult. The hardest way to come off is to stop taking the whole dose suddenly. Many people, not realizing that they are tranquillizer dependent, try this; however, when they suffer from withdrawal symptoms and panic they go back to the full dose again.

Sally suffered from depression after her divorce and over the next seven years experienced a whole range of treatment, from ECT, anti-depressant drugs and tranquillizers to group therapy in a psychiatric hospital, after which she was convinced she was severely mentally ill. This idea was reinforced when she started to experience bad panic attacks, phobias and general anxiety which she had never experienced before. Apart from the psychological symptoms, Sally suffered from digestive disorders, migraine headaches, vertigo and skin troubles – all of which were investigated in hospital, the tests proving negative. When her GP came to the conclusion that tranquillizers were at the root of the problem Sally decided to give them up on the spot. Although she experienced numerous withdrawal symptoms she insisted that none were as bad as the problems she had had while on the drugs. Luckily Sally had the support of a helpful GP and a local self-help group.

Most people find it easier to come off drugs gradually and over a reasonable period of time. Going slowly, they can call a halt at any particular level and stay at that level until they feel ready to go a bit further. RELEASE says that it is difficult to estimate how long it might take for your body to be completely free of the effects of tranquillizers.

So many people have taken different types of tranquillizers and other drugs in various combinations and quantities, for varying lengths of time. The problems for which the tranquillizers were prescribed in the first place also vary, and some were worse than others. Some may have been partially resolved by tranquillizer use, and some may not.

The important thing to understand is that you will get there in the end. Seek all the help you can from your GP and organizations such as RELEASE and CITA, and local support groups where there are members who will know how you feel and will be able to offer help and comfort.

In general, it is safe to say that tranquillizers are not the answer – particularly in the long term. Research is currently going on into a new drug that, it is claimed, will halt a panic attack in a couple of minutes. It is said to have no harmful side effects and the fact that it is taken only when needed means that it should not become addictive. However, the drug, called Bretazenil, will not be on the market for another two years, and it remains to be seen whether its researchers' claims will be substantiated.

# 5
# A LOOK AT SOME
# ALTERNATIVE APPROACHES

These days people are becoming disillusioned about the conventional treatment available for the treatment of anxiety states. Much of what is available is unsatisfactory, often due to the lack of empathy on the part of the medical profession. The doctor-patient relationship is hardly likely to flourish when the average time for a consultation is five minutes. Many are turning to alternative forms of treatment in the hope that they may find a sympathetic therapist who will listen to them in the first place, show that they actually appear to understand the problem and suggest sensible ways of tackling it.

There are many roads to explore on the way to recovery and there is no doubt that many people have made some progress when changing direction. Cynics will say that the patient was probably on the point of recovery in any case, and the fact that a different approach appeared to be successful just happened to be a happy coincidence. In the past, many Open Door members and, more recently, PAX members were enthusiastic about trying anything which might improve their emotional and physical state and help them to help themselves in a positive way.

We will consider some of the therapies and remedies that have been tried by patients seeking relief from anxiety symptoms and phobias, particularly agoraphobia. Among them you might find the one that helps you.

# ACUPUNCTURE

The word acupuncture comes from the Latin words *acus* (needle) and *punctura* (to prick). It is used to describe a technique in which needles are used to puncture the skin at certain defined points in order to restore the balance of energy which acupuncturists believe is essential to good health.

In the West we look on the body as a piece of machinery which needs constant maintenance and repair. When something goes wrong, we rush it into the workshop (doctor's surgery) to be fitted with spare parts: fuel, lubricants and various nuts and bolts which will enable it to keep going until another bit needs attention. To the ancient Chinese, the human being was a living thing, not just a machine but 'a field for the action and interaction of the invisible forces of life'. Dr Felix Mann, author of *Acupuncture, Cure of Many Diseases* also points out:

> The harmony of these vital powers within was revealed by the health of the whole body, their disharmony by disease, their disappearance by its death. So the aim of the Chinese doctor was to correct the imbalance of the vital forces in the body. Once the harmonious interplay of these forces had been resolved the patient himself was able to overcome his weakness.

The flow of nervous energy through the body was described by the Chinese as *chi* – the energy of life; something like a wave of electricity running along the nerve. They called the principal nerve endings acupuncture points and in Chinese literature there are descriptions of about a thousand such points classified into twelve main groups. All the points in any one of these groups are joined by a line which is known as a meridian. *Chi* was regarded as a river which flowed through the meridians. If the body was diseased or disturbed, a blockage occurred and the flow of *chi* slowed down. The acupuncture needle would remove the blockage, opening up the channel so that once more *chi* was able to flow through it.

Most people who have nervous problems are considered to have some underactivity of the kidneys. If you consider this, you will realize that one of the symptoms of fear is a need to urinate. In these cases the acupuncturist would treat the points on the kidney meridian which runs down the lower parts of the arms and legs. The needles would be inserted and, during the ten minutes or so while they are left in place, they may be twirled from time to time by the therapist in order to increase the flow of *chi*. During this time the patient might feel a slight tingling sensation – a positive feeling, proving that the system was being 'tuned up'.

I have had a number of enthusiastic reports from acupunctured panic or anxiety sufferers:

I was so nervous when I went for my first session and even more so when the doctor told me that he could not cure my agoraphobia. That was the whole reason for my consulting him and I was almost ready to abandon the whole thing. There was a slight tingling in my forearms and down my legs and I immediately felt much better – for some reason I had expected the needles to be put in my head! I think that was the main reason for my apprehension beforehand. The needles were left in place for about ten minutes after which time I felt relaxed and rested – though a bit disconcerted to find that for several hours after the treatment I felt 'electric shocks' in my legs.

I have been regularly for treatment for six months and my anxiety state is greatly improved. The agoraphobia bit I am tackling with a programme drawn up with the doctor. We discuss my progress before each treatment session and when I am relaxed and doing my pincushion act we plan the next part of my programme and the obstacles I propose to tackle.

I really feel that acupuncture is working for me particularly as the doctor understands the agoraphobia condition so well.

Acupuncture does not depend solely on correct diagnosis and accurate positioning of needles during treatment, with the patient as passive onlooker while everything is done for her. With the anxiety damped down, there is still a lot of hard work to do.

# AROMATHERAPY

The essential oils or essences of plants are thought to be the very personality – the hormones – of the plant itself. They can be taken internally, inhaled or massaged through the skin. It has been found that much more passes through the skin than we previously thought possible; in France many drugs are applied to the skin surface and thus are gradually absorbed into the system. Robert Tisserand, an expert on aromatherapy, states that some oils are taken up by specific body organs, while others are distributed more generally.

After the patient's case history has been taken, the therapist selects the suitable essential oils and, in a carrier oil, like apricot kernel or wheatgerm, massages them along the spine. The oils may also be massaged into the temples and various other pulse points. A suitable and individual blend of oils will be prepared for you, and you may be asked to use them in your bath, in a vapourizer (lightbulb rings are good), for massage purposes or, very rarely, taken internally.

Maggie Tisserand, in *Aromatherapy for Women*, says that essential oils are the natural alternative to tranquillizers and suggests, among others, that a few drops of geranium or lavender oil in the bath will reduce physical and mental tension and harmonize troubled emotions:

> If you have an acute attack of depression . . . then a bath in *ylang-ylang* or *clary sage* will go a long way towards making you feel better. *Jasmine oil*, although rather costly to buy, is a really excellent depression-fighter. It lifts the spirits and makes you feel really good.

Sandalwood and bergamot are also good.

According to Robert Tisserand, essential oils sprayed from an aerosol can be used in the treatment of patients suffering from anxiety or depression: 'The effect of odours on the emotions has been known for centuries, but it is only in the last thirty years or so that we have begun to realize the healing potential of this deep, inherent response to fragrance.'

An Open Door member comments:

Besides my extra-strong mints which I always carry with me . . . I
have a phial of basil oil to smell if I should come over faint . . . I
also have a pillow filled with hop flowers to help me sleep properly.
I believe this is very effective. Hop or herb pillows also make lovely
presents to buy or even make yourself.

# BACH FLOWER REMEDIES

Bach Flower Remedies are prepared from the flowers of wild plants,
bushes and trees and none of them is harmful or habit-forming.

They are used, *not directly* for physical complaints, but for the
sufferer's worry, apprehension, hopelessness, irritability, etc.,
because these states of mind or moods not only hinder recovery of
health and retard convalescence, but are generally accepted as primary causes of sickness and disease.

Bach handbook

In 1930 Dr Edward Bach, a Harley Street consultant, bacteri-
ologist and homeopath gave up his practice and returned to his
native Wales to search for flowers and trees that have healing
powers. Dr Bach discovered thirty-eight herbal remedies which
he developed from various plants, claiming that these could
alter the disharmonies of personality and emotional states. He
classified human mental conditions into seven major groups:
apprehension; uncertainty and indecision; loneliness; insuf-
ficient interest in present circumstances; over-sensitiveness to
ideas and influence; despondency and despair; over-care for the
welfare of others.

The flowers are preserved in pure brandy and may be taken
internally (four drops in a small glass of water) or applied
externally to the temples, wrists or lips. In an emergency, a few
drops may be placed directly on the tongue.

Remedies suitable for anxiety sufferers would include:

*Aspen*            For apprehension and foreboding. Fears of
                   *unknown* origin.

| | |
|---|---|
| *Rock Rose* | Terror, extreme fear or panic. |
| *White Chestnut* | Persistent unwanted thoughts. Preoccupation with some worry or episode. |
| *Larch* | Despondency due to lack of self-confidence; expectation of failure, so fails to make the attempt . . . |

In particular, Rescue Remedy, a blend of Rock Rose, Clematis, Impatiens, Cherry Plum and Star of Bethlehem flowers is recommended in cases of panic.

At least five sufferers I know swear by the Bach Remedies, claiming that they have been helped to find peace of mind; each one has been making considerable progress towards overcoming his fears.


# BIOFEEDBACK

Using a special electronic meter, it is possible to learn to measure – and, with practice, control – your anxiety level. Anxiety causes certain changes in the body, such as an increased heart rate and a galvanic skin response (GSR). You will have noticed that when you get nervous your hands become clammy; the biofeedback instrument can measure these levels of perspiration and show the amount of stress you are experiencing. There are some very simple meters which are suitable for anyone to use, while others are extremely complicated and able to monitor brainwaves.

The biofeedback instrument itself will not reduce tension or anxiety, but, used in conjunction with relaxation exercises, the individual can soon learn how to bring down their anxiety level.

The simplest gadget of all is a small card which, it is claimed, can be used to measure your state of tension. The black circle in the centre changes colour to tell you whether you are totally calm and relaxed, or tense and agitated. Possibly this is a gimmick which will appeal to some anxiety-prone people who could carry it around and, when feeling their panic level rising, reduce it by concentrating on making the black circle change to a calming blue!

# BIORHYTHMS

From the moment of birth, our 'body clocks' start to operate and our individual rhythms are established. One expert holds that 'When a person is born, the trauma of leaving the safe and warm confines of the mother's womb sets in motion a series of three cycles which will continue to recur at regular intervals until death.'

We each have a physical cycle of twenty-three days, an emotional cycle of twenty-eight days and an intellectual cycle of thirty-three days. If charted on a graph, each circle forms a wave pattern, and it is while crossing the middle of each cycle – either from high to low or from low to high – that the individual experiences an unstable or 'critical period'; this is more significant if the 'critical' periods of two or three cycles happen to coincide on the same day. It is during these critical periods that the individual is more illness or accident prone; hence, knowledge of one's own cycle may be useful in making decisions, for example, or in knowing when to take care to avoid stressful occasions.

Biorhythm charts are easily obtainable, and there are also small pocket calculators on which you can work out your biorhythms by keying in your birth date and reading off your critical days.

# CLINICAL NUTRITION

Clinical Nutrition is also called Dietary Therapy, and, as its name suggests, is a therapy based on a sound diet and sensible nutrition. The clinical nutritionist will go through your diet with you, suggesting improvements, and give you a series of tests to discover which, if any, deficiencies you are suffering from. Then, a series of dietary supplements may be prescribed, which will take care of any imbalance within your body.

In today's world, it is virtually impossible to get from our food all the vitamins, minerals, amino acids, etc. necessary to complete wellbeing. With over-processing, rushed ripening and production and various additives, and pesticides, many of the nutrients that once constituted a good percentage of whole food are now severely depleted. Therefore, unless you eat entirely whole, organic foods, chances are you are suffering from a deficiency.

We discussed earlier that panic can certainly be biological, and deficiencies in, for instance, the B vitamins may have an enormous impact on your nervous system. Allergies may also cause unusual physiological and psychological reactions to things, and a careful analysis of your diet may alleviate a number of the symptoms.

There are a number of herbal remedies for anxiety, including damiana, myo-inositol, St John's Wort, Valerian and Kava Kava, while depression can be relieved by magnesium, oats, Vitamins C and B6, as well as licorice and yohimbine.

The list of herbal and dietary remedies for panic- and stress-related symptoms is endless, and it is certainly worth a visit to your nearest clinical nutritionist or medical herbalist to see what's on offer.

## DANCE THERAPY

An Open Door member writes:

> When I am wound up the one way I can find relief is to switch on some music and dance around the house. Moving rhythmically eases tension and I feel quite uplifted after dancing to my favourite tunes. I particularly like Scottish country dance music, even if I do finish up puffed and exhausted.

Many people go to dancing classes simply to unwind; others go for social reasons or as a means of keeping fit and lessening the physical effects of tension – especially good for anxiety sufferers or agoraphobics who quite often do not take enough exercise. Dancing as a therapy in tribal communities is used to lead the participants into a trance state, the music and drumming encouraging an orgy of movement which develops into convulsions as the witch doctor and the rest of the tribe become possessed by healing spirits.

In the civilized world this tradition lingered on for some time. Fits – even outbreaks of mass hysteria such as the dancing mania of the early Middle Ages – were taken to be divine visitations and had their own patron, St Vitus. But when such fits came to be regarded as a form of mental illness, dancing survived like so much else only as a ritual or pastime, purged of its therapeutic content.

There have always been those who have felt that dance has a place in therapy, not just as an exercise for the body but also as an outlet for the emotions.

## HEALING

One anxiety sufferer found healing the best cure for her illness:

I had not met the minister before he came to my house that evening. I had heard that other people suffering from nervous illness had been helped by him and though I had been house-bound for three years I just had the feeling that this man would be my salvation. When he sat down and took my hands in his I burst into tears. For half an hour the minister sat with me, praying for my recovery, and gradually I became more and more certain that I *would* get better.

Next day I went out with my daughter. Not just to the front gate or to the corner of the road, but right round the block. I kept saying, 'I'm not afraid any more, I know I can do it.' I now go out *every day* much to the delight of my family. Flashes of memory of the old terrors sometimes disturb me but I put them to the back of my mind and tell myself that everyone feels a little peculiar at times and I am just as normal as anyone else.

I feel that God meant me to get better at that moment. He showed me what it was like to be able to go out and enjoy the world and I could not let him down by ever backsliding.

In many cultures it is accepted that the laying on of hands can effect a healing process. Healing simply makes use of a kind of empathy as the main source of healing power, though many hand healers now assume that there is some bio-electromagnetic element in healing.

Basically there are two kinds of healer. The spiritual healer works on the principle that whatever one believes can be made to happen – helping the patient to 'tune-in' to his God, Life Force or Higher Power. Once this happens, he is open to receive the healing force.

Spirit healing includes contact with the world of disincarnate spirits through clairvoyants, spiritualists and other psychics. There are many charlatans in this group and I hesitate to suggest that agoraphobes dabble in this field, because a bad experience might upset an already over-sensitized nervous system and thus cause a great deal of distress. I cannot deny, however, that I have known people to make a spectacular recovery after consulting a psychic healer. Ensure you contact the National Federation of Spiritual Healers (address at the back of the book) who have, generally, only those truly gifted healers on their books. They will recommend someone near you. Many healers do not accept payment for their help.

The most famous healer in Britain in recent times was Harry Edwards. He claimed that all forms of spiritual healing come from God and that healers are obeying Jesus's order, also from God, to heal the sick. They do not themselves possess healing powers, but are the instruments through whom the divine plan is carried out. Healers are chosen because they have the capacity to channel the healing force through themselves into other people. When a healing occurs, therefore, it is not an indication of divine favour; it is simply a further proof that such healing is available to all and sundry, given the individual's desire to *be* healed.

Another anxiety sufferer found spiritual healing cured her of her long-held problems:

74

I was determined to go to the meeting as I had heard that this healer had performed unbelievable miracles for other people like myself who had suffered from nerves for most of my adult life. My husband took me, although he was very sceptical and I think he was afraid that I would be so disappointed I would just give up completely. I had to have a chair by the open door at the back of the hall – difficult because there were so many people grouped around there and somebody made a joke about claustrophobia.

What happened is a bit of a blur. I found the whole thing so emotional I couldn't stop crying . . . I had thought that people would have to go up on to the stage to him, but he came down to the audience, sat with different people and talked to them and stroked their heads. There was no excited hysteria as I had expected, just a sort of quiet joy, as people stood, walked, flexed muscles that had been locked. I just wish I had been able to have a clear picture instead of sitting and crying and so wrapped up in myself. When he came to me I managed to stop crying and whispered that I had been suffering from agoraphobia for so many years I was afraid I would never get better. He put his hands on my shoulders and looked into my eyes and said, 'God wants you to get better, if *you* want to get better you will.'

'At least you've stopped her crying,' said my husband.

I find I am more relaxed and have a wonderful feeling of peace these days. I haven't managed to do anything very spectacular, but I know it is only a matter of time before I can do all the things I have missed over the 'Aggie' years. If I happen to feel a bit down I say to myself, 'God wants me to get better – I want to get better.'

And as we all know, half the battle is maintaining one's belief in the possibility of recovery.

# HOMOEOPATHY

Wherever she goes, the Queen takes a battered black box full of medicines many chemists have never heard of . . . The Queen . . . uses arsenic for sneezing, or an upset stomach, onion for a runny nose, and anemone when someone is down in the dumps after an illness . . .

The Queen's interest in homoeopathy – a system of 'alternative' medicine developed at the end of the eighteenth century – stems from childhood. Her father, the late King George VI, used to treat both his daughters this way.

James Whitaker, London *Daily Star*, 1st February 1980

Homoeopathy is based on the principle that a disease does not attack the body but rather is the body's method of curing itself of something which is wrong. Samuel Hahnemann, a German doctor in the early nineteenth century, believed that any substance which actually induces symptoms similar to those of a particular disease is probably stimulating the disease-fighting systems in the body and so is able to cure the condition. Homoeopathy is based on the theory that 'like cures like', that is, by administering small quantities of whatever is causing the ailment, your body will call upon its natural defences to cure the ailment. For example, a small quantity of an allergen may be given to someone suffering from hay fever, forcing his or her natural defences to fight it off, building them up in the process. Hahnemann taught that the smaller the potency of the drug administered, the more easily it is absorbed into the sick body which would reject a stronger dose. The substances from which the homoeopathic drugs are obtained would in many cases be exceedingly poisonous if taken in anything but minute quantities. In the diluted form in which they are administered, they area absolutely safe, even for pregnant women and children.

This form of medicine is available under the National Health Service and the Faculty of Homoeopathy in London is recognized in law just like all the other medical faculties. Any general practitioner can write a prescription for a homoeopathic patient and many chemists stock homoeopathic medicines. There are also lay homoeopaths practising in this country who are not qualified doctors but may be osteopaths, acupuncturists or other practitioners of alternative medicine who use homoeopathic remedies in conjunction with their own specific type of therapy.

Homoeopathy is 'whole person' medicine. During the initial consultation a homoeopathic doctor will note down a detailed history, taking into account the patient's lifestyle, personality, temperament and even general likes and dislikes. He will not concentrate on symptoms alone, because two patients with exactly the same symptoms may need to be treated very differently.

Homoeopathic remedies are widely available and 'first aid kits' can be purchased in chemists' shops. They are cheap and safe, but homoeopaths feel that anyone wishing to experiment should learn something about the subject generally before doing so.

The appeal of homoeopathy to the anxiety or panic attack patient lies not only in consulting someone who may be able to prescribe safe drugs to help alleviate anxiety symptoms, but also in the knowledge that the practitioner thoroughly understands the background to her condition and is able to offer sympathetic and practical advice aimed at overcoming background physical causes that may be aggravating the problem.

# HYPNOSIS

This is one of the first of the alternative therapies that anxiety sufferers turn to – unfortunately, usually in the misguided hope that they can be 'put to sleep' and wake completely free of their symptoms. It's important to understand that *nothing* can do this; the important thing to learn is what you yourselves have to do.

Hypnosis is not sleep. Many people can be hypnotized and remain wide awake and conscious of their surroundings, and it is quite possible for the subjects to resist and reject ideas and suggestions made to them by the hypnotist. Though hypnosis can be helpful in achieving a state of complete relaxation, it is difficult to hypnotize someone who is excessively anxious – the type of person who needs to relax most of all.

An Open Door member described her experiences after a friend had recommended her own hypnotherapist who had proved very helpful. She was apprehensive because she had a dread of anaesthetics and felt that hypnosis might have a similar effect – that she would not be in control of her own body and mind. After the first two sessions, she wrote to the Open Door newsletter to describe her experiences:

> During the first session, she (the hypnotherapist) took my case history and we discussed whether there might be any deeper causes for my agoraphobia. I told her about my fears and my anaesthetic phobia and she was very reassuring, explaining that there was nothing for me to worry about . . . I was then tested to find out if I would respond to hypnosis. I was told that my eyes were becoming tired and beginning to close and then she asked me to concentrate on the hand I used least. As she told me my hand was getting lighter and rising up I realized that was exactly what was happening, after which I was told to relax deeper and deeper.
>
> My next visit found me much less nervous. The hypnotherapist asked me to lie down, breathe deeply and think of a time and place when I had felt tranquil and happy. Again I became more and more relaxed and was told at the end of the session that I had actually been in a light trance. I must admit I was a little disappointed when told not to expect my symptoms to disappear as a result of hypnosis, but now realize that it can help me gain confidence to tackle the agoraphobia problems.

Another woman had been agoraphobic for eight years, during four years of which she had been virtually house-bound. Psychiatric treatment and drugs had helped a little, but she felt that progress should be faster and was lucky enough to find a psychiatrist who also practised hypnosis at her local NHS hospital:

> I didn't get put to sleep and feel wonderful as I had been led to believe, though I can't say the experience was unpleasant. But next morning I felt marvellous – like I hadn't felt for years. I could hardly believe it. I felt like this for three days and did all sorts of things I hadn't done for ages . . . then the effect wore off and I was back where I started until I went for treatment number two.
>
> My second appointment was at a bad time; I had sinus trouble and was feeling really low. But I went and again I benefited. Could this really be me throwing 'Aggie' off so easily?
>
> On my third visit the hypnotherapist took me through a panic. He put me under hypnosis and when I was completely relaxed told me I was now getting into a panic. He kept telling me that the

panic was getting worse, while I had to imagine I was in the supermarket. Then when I felt I would get up and run out, he said he would count to ten and the panic would get worse and worse. At ten I thought I'd go really mad but he then calmed me down, still in the supermarket situation. He made me feel really calm, then woke me up. My goodness, was I exhausted! However I got up slowly and came out feeling on top of the world and was able to go out with my husband for the rest of the evening.

It was now a regular thing to feel completely free of 'Aggie' for three days after treatment, but after session three on day four I suddenly became very weepy and stayed like this until my next appointment. My psychiatrist assured me that this was a normal side effect of hypnosis for someone like myself who had repressed my feelings for years. Having hypnosis opens up the subconscious mind and things that have been buried in the past come floating to the surface. He explained that it was good for me to be weepy as my emotions were being liberated.

The next time I had treatment I was even more weepy for a day but as the week wore on I began to feel better. After the fifth session I began to notice how much more relaxed I was generally and was able to go into crowded places. On Easter Sunday morning I went to church. That really was a big step forward, it was also the first Bank Holiday I can remember ever going out and enjoying myself. I could hardly believe that five ten-minute sessions of hypnosis had made such a difference to my life.

Since Easter I have had three more sessions. My only fear now is that the effects may not last, but I am assured that because I have learnt to relax and my confidence has increased a hundred per cent that I could cope with panic if it does arise again.

On contacting these women about two years later I found that though neither could say that they were completely 'cured' both said that they felt much better and most importantly their confidence had improved so much they were able to face up to their problems and keep anxiety under control.

The importance of hypnosis is that it helps to produce a state of deep relaxation which, in conjunction with supportive psychotherapy and behavioural techniques, such as graduated exposure therapy, will help the patient to understand and overcome her fears. On its own, hypnosis is usually of little help.

Too many people are grasping at straws hoping that their fears will just melt away and many give up when they realize how much they themselves have to contribute to their recovery.

Unfortunately, it is the hope of an easy cure which causes sufferers to put themselves at risk, in the hands of unqualified practitioners. There are many lay therapists who are excellent and have helped a number of people but it is a good rule – if you are proposing to consult a hypnotherapist – to do so only on the recommendation of another patient who has experience of their technique. Alternatively, you can contact the British Society of Dental and Medical Hypnosis or the Association of Hypnotists and Psychotherapists (see page 202 for details), who keep registers of practitioners.

# OSMOTHERAPY

Scientists have recognized and begun to harness the power of certain fragrances to alter mood, to stimulate and sedate, to cure insomnia and to treat all kinds of complaints. In fact, it was around the year 1580 that Montaigne wrote in his *Essay on Smells*:

> Physicians might make greater use of scents than they do for I have often noticed that they cause changes in me and act on my spirits . . . which makes me agree with the theory that the introduction of incense and perfume into the churches . . . was for the purpose of raising our spirits and of exciting and purifying our senses, the better to fit us for contemplation.

It is now accepted that certain scents can be as powerful as prescription tranquillizers. Dr John King, Consultant Psychiatrist at Smallwood Dat Hospital in Redditch, Worcestershire, has been using certain fragrances to reduce anxiety in his patients. Dr King feels that conventional drug therapy is rarely sufficient for people suffering from anxiety. It is now known that the parts of the brain which control mood and emotions are closely linked to the sense of smell, and that the receptors in the brain are well away from those parts which deal with speech and logic. So it appears that our response to smell is more emotional than intellectual.

We also know that there is a close correlation between the action of fragrance molecules and that of mood-altering drugs, such as tranquillizers and anti-depressants.

Dr King has found that even a synthetic seaside fragrance which he concocted himself has a head start on many other relaxing scents, purely on the strength of its association with memories of carefree holidays and a sense of wellbeing.

Professor George Dodd of Warwick University has produced a therapeutic scented sponge in a small cassette to be carried in the handbag or pocket. Marketed under the name 'Osmone' it has been developed as an alternative to conventional tranquil lizers and it is claimed that a couple of sniffs are all that is needed for instant relaxation.

On the basis of their research, osmotherapy is probably worth investigating further.

## PAST LIVES THERAPY

If we have souls which survive death, or if reincarnation exists, it would not be surprising if traces of our past lives should periodically filter down into a present life, causing mental or emotional disturbance. Past lives therapy is based on the assumption that some disorders arise because of past lives burrowing their way into an individual's subconscious and that these psychic intrusions may need to be brought to the surface.

I attended a workshop held by a psychoanalyst Dr Roger Woolger who believes many mental and physical problems stem from events which happened not in this life but in some previous existence. Past lives therapy is a controversial treatment which has taken America by storm and Dr Woolger is now teaching British therapists the art of regressing patients under hypnosis to a previous life so that past traumas may be exposed and dealt with in the context of the subject's current experiences.

I watched one woman who had volunteered to be regressed

in front of an audience. She suffered from recurring panic attacks and also had painful arthritis in her neck, which she permanently held on one side. Whilst in a light trance she kept touching her throat and complaining of an iron collar and a chain which was stapled to a wall.

'Keep them away from me, I'm not like them,' she kept shrieking, and we gathered that she was in a mad house in a previous century, that she herself was perfectly sane and the other inmates tormented her, submitting her to verbal and physical abuse until they actually killed her.

Pretty harrowing stuff but the subject, when brought out of hypnosis, quickly recovered from her distress and became quite calm – obviously believing Dr Woolger when he told her that after a few sessions of psychotherapy she could be cured.

We were told of a severely agoraphobic woman who had been completely housebound. When she consulted Dr Woolger she told him she was afraid of people looking at her and sizing her up. Under hypnosis she remembered a miserable life as a slave and being prodded by slave owners and checked for breeding purposes. When that life was brought to the surface and the patient understood that there was nothing to be afraid of any more, she was soon on the way to recovery.

Over the years I have had letters from a number of people who were convinced their phobias had some bearing on a past life. One woman wrote to me:

I am presently working on the idea that I was a nun some five hundred years ago. You may laugh, but I am quite convinced about this. For a serious indiscretion I was banished from my convent and left to face the outside world alone. Unable to cope with this I committed suicide, but the trauma has affected all my later incarnations.

Are these experiences real or imaginary? Many psychotherapists are practising regression and at the workshop I met many of their patients who are convinced that they are on the right track. 'Even if it is my imagination,' one woman told me, 'it gives me a reason for my fears [claustrophobia and a fear of being suffocated because a wall fell on her in a previous life] and I can work through these with my therapist.'

In the spirit of research I decided to try this out for myself (privately, not in front of an audience). Perhaps I would discover the reason for the anxieties and phobias of my youth. Perhaps I would also discover why I managed to shed them.

I spent a relaxing three hours with the psychotherapist but we unearthed only a rather boring young woman called Maggie. Daughter of an East Anglian farmer she became a teacher but decided she didn't really like children. She was interested only in herself and in acquiring knowledge. She set out with a girl friend for America but the sailing ship she was in was sunk in a storm at sea and Maggie was killed by a falling spar.

This story which unravelled before me rather like a film left me totally unmoved by Maggie's fate and certainly no way nearer to learning about past fears.

Perhaps you'll find a reason for your fears in the analysis of a past life. For some, this therapy has proved most rewarding, if somewhat off the beaten track!

## PYRAMID HEALING

I spend half an hour each day sitting beneath my pyramid structure, cross-legged and with my eyes shut. I cannot tell you what this does for me in the way of relaxation. At the end of the half-hour all my tensions have gone and I feel quite euphoric.

I know it looks weird and my family tease me, though I have caught my teenage daughter trying it out though she explained somewhat shamefacedly that it was just for a joke. No one can deny that my agoraphobia is much improved and I go out now with scarcely any trouble; if I feel panicky feelings bubbling up I am better able to cope with them. My husband insists that it is just superstition, but I know there is more to it than that.

Do pyramids really have some special powers? For the past fifty years men have been researching this possibility, based on the theory that certain electromagnetic waves are concentrated and condensed by the particular configuration of a pyramid.

Experiments have shown that that particular shape seems to attract more of the earth's magnetic forces than we would expect, and the benefit derived from pyramids may have something to do with the balance of negative and positive ions in the air. At Leningrad University, the Russians are carrying out extensive research into pyramid energies at a large pyramid research department. A Czechoslovakian radio technician patented a cardboard pyramid-shaped razor-blade sharpener which prolongs the life of a normal blade for anything up to four months. Other experiments have shown that the taste of food can be improved if kept under a pyramidal structure and that plant growth can also be affected. It is possible to buy pyramid kits of all sizes in the form of a metal frame structure, and the literature is certainly fascinating.

Whether it serves to calm you, or simply to provide a respite from day-to-day problems, it might be worth a try.

## REFLEXOLOGY

This therapy is based on the principle that each part of the body is reflected at certain points on the feet and hands. Massage of these points – or simply pressure – activates the vital force (much like the *chi* of acupuncture) of each organ, restoring flow of energy to the body.

Reflexology is used as a treatment for a number of common complaints, including stress, headaches and breathing troubles. Perhaps a breathing disorder is at the root of your panic attacks!

Reflexology can be done at home, or by a registered practitioner and can be used to overcome fainting, nausea, fear, fatigue, insomnia, dizziness, drug addiction and depression, among other things.

## SHIATSU AND ACUPRESSURE

Acupressure is a form of acupuncture without needles – literally, 'finger pressure'. Shiatsu is the Japanese form of this, though during treatment pressure can be applied not only by the fingers and thumbs but by the palm or heel of the hand, a knee, an elbow or the feet.

In Japan, Shiatsu has always been a kind of family therapy, a remedial massage performed by one member of the family on another. The pressure is designed to stimulate the acupuncture points and meridians, to alter the energy flow in the body either to sedate or tone them up.

A good Shiatsu practitioner can make the patient feel elated or sedated, depending on what he does and which meridians he stimulates. This therapy is particularly suitable for a nervous patient who may be worried about needles (although they are entirely painless).

A form of acupressure massage which anyone can use on themselves is known as 'Do-in'. When the subject has learned the basic acupuncture points, she can work along the meridians or just concentrate on the parts which appear to bring relief from symptoms. There are many books which have instructions on do-it-yourself acupressure, and recently available are tiny magnets which are fixed over the acupuncture points with adhesive plasters, the idea being that they provide a constant pressure and can also be pressed more firmly from time to time in order to increase the energy flow through the meridians.

## SMILE THERAPY

Way back in 1906 a French psychologist called Waynbaum published a book in which he stated that the facial muscles act as ligatures on the blood vessels and regulate blood flow to the brain. The blood flow in turn influences how we feel. The theory he developed held that emotions often follow on from facial expressions, rather than always preceding them. Waynbaum suggested that all overt emotional reactions such as blushing, sobbing and weeping are closely tied to vascular processes. Weeping and laughter affect the blood circulation, whether positively or negatively, and facial expressions play an important part in this process.

'Why is it,' he asked, 'that smiling and laughter are always associated with happiness and joy?' He suggested that blood flow to the brain – which is the physiological result of smiling and laughter – is associated with a healthy body and a positive mood. In this case if you *make* yourself smile you will probably feel happier.

Depressive moods and expressions, by contrast, result in a decreased flow of blood to the brain. This, in time, can lead to actual ill health. So people who constantly go around with a gloomy expression on their faces are causing a permanent decrease of blood to the brain. This means that the brain is not receiving proper nutrients and is not working at optimum levels.

Waynbaum says that laughing must be a healthy activity because improved circulation is a good thing. Laughter is rather like taking an oxygen bath: the cells and tissues all receive an increased supply of oxygen.

'Many behavioural problems could be averted if people were persuaded of the importance of smiling,' writes Liz Hodgkinson in her book *Smile Therapy*. It would be less easy to become caught in a vicious downward circle of depression and despair if facial expressions were kept positive. People imagine this is difficult to do but in fact it isn't. Once it is understood that facial expressions really do affect emotions, smile therapy can be put into practice!

There is a very logical reason why people who smile a lot seem to have the secret of eternal youth. It's not anything magic but simply to do with the muscles involved in pulling different facial expressions. In smiling, only one major muscle is used whereas in the expression of all the negative emotions, such as anxiety, fear, disgust and sadness, very many more muscles are involved. For every facial expression except smiling, the face has to be contorted. The more the face is twisted up into unhappy expressions the sooner those wrinkles will turn into ageing, permanent lines.

After discussing these theories in the PAX newsletter a number of members wrote in to say they were practising smile therapy.

I didn't realize how glum my face looked in repose until I surprised myself in front of a mirror. I am making a conscious effort to confront my reflection and smile at it several times a day. 'Are you feeling happy?' asked my husband (hopefully). 'No, but I'm trying to look happy,' I said. He laughed. I laughed, but it hit home that usually I don't smile much and look as miserable as I feel.

Another reader noted:

I have found that it is important to smile with my mouth slightly open, otherwise I am inclined to grit my teeth and this increases tension. I also keep telling myself: Look happy and you will be happy.

Crying and laughter both release tensions, but laughter is much better for you and is a quicker, more effective way of relaxing than meditation, exercise or drugs. Laughter can make you feel quite weak because it is a muscle relaxant and counteracts the 'fight or flight' feelings. It's also probably the cheapest therapy on offer – and you can do it in the privacy of your own home!

# YOGA

Yoga is chiefly concerned with exercises designed to improve posture and breathing, on the principle that these lead not only to better physical health but also to greater self-confidence and serenity because stress and tension are removed. The yoga postures range from sitting positions to movements aimed at toning the body and making it supple. Each posture has three main parts – a bodily movement, a mental control process and a specific control of respiration. Great emphasis is put on correct breathing.

As we know, people suffering from panic or anxiety are tense and inclined to breathe in a shallow and irregular way, so a yoga instructor will start off by getting the subject to breathe correctly. When the body is calm and relaxed, the life forces are more in harmony.

I have to admit that Open Door members who managed to get to yoga classes may not always have appreciated the deeper meanings behind the movements, but they certainly benefited from the social side of the sessions. On the whole yoga proved helpful in a number of ways and one Open Door lady eventually became a yoga instructress herself.

It is not advisable to try 'do-it-yourself' yoga unless you have attended classes in the first place.

## ANYTHING GOES

The value of any remedy, however odd it may appear, is that the patient finds someone who will listen sympathetically and spend time discussing the problem – the time which an NHS doctor so often lacks.

Some of the therapies discussed in this chapter may seem a bit unusual, but each one of them has been tried by sufferers whom I have interviewed or who have written to me.

James Foster, an Open Door member, had an interesting story to tell about his experiences. He wrote:

While I was living in West Africa, I was still struggling with agora-phobia though disinclined to discuss it with anyone, even my own doctor who was a close personal friend.

More in the spirit of anthropological research (I told myself) than in any real hope of a cure, I decided to consult the local shaman (witch doctor).

In the rather spooky atmosphere of his home I began to wonder what I was letting myself in for, having recently seen a James Bond film in which there was a colourful but unnerving voodoo ceremony. I need not have worried; though weird there was nothing too dramatic about my treatment. I had to sit crosslegged on the floor while my 'therapist' placed a selection of dried-up herbs in my outstretched hands. I felt a bit of a ninny sitting there while he circled about me crooning and chanting under his breath. Now was the time to have a full-scale panic attack, I thought, experiencing an escalation of anxiety and looking around the claustrophobic chamber for the nearest escape route.

I stayed calm, not wanting to make an exhibition of myself – it seemed somehow ungrateful. The shaman flopped down in front of me and produced a pile of ashes out of a leather bag (ashes of what? I wondered), shuffling with them, spreading them on the floor and drawing signs amongst them with a stick.

That was the end of the first session; no noticeable improvement in my agoraphobia during the next few days and I felt a bit of a fool when I thought about it, but I went back for another session and followed up with two more. It seemed ungrateful to admit defeat, especially as he had offered to call in a second opinion, but not knowing what the 'consultant' might suggest in the way of treatment (a sacrificial cockerel and a few human bones to juggle with, perhaps) I decided to terminate the consultations and proffered my thanks to the shaman who was now richer by one watch, two shirts and a pair of shoes.

I decided to postpone any further treatment until I returned home to England.

In a letter some months later James wrote that he had returned to England and married. He felt more relaxed and able to cope with his agoraphobia, which seemed to be receding. This he put down to 'determination to win and a quirky sense of humour which encouraged him to see the funny side of any experience, however grim, and enabled him to put things into perspective'.

There are no rules for what will and will not work. Whatever feels most comfortable to you will probably be most helpful. Perhaps experimentation is an option for some sufferers.

# THE COST OF EXPERIMENTATION . . . IS IT WORTH IT?

Alternative medicines (aside from homeopathy) are not subsidized by the National Health Service and this may be the first time that the anxiety sufferer has ever had to pay for treatment. The greatest difference between private and NHS treatment is the amount of time the practitioner spends with the patient. Appointments will last probably between thirty minutes and three hours and the patient receives completely individual attention, based on a detailed analysis of almost every aspect of his or her character, physiology and mental state. Treatments can be free (for instance, some spiritual healers do not charge), or cost as much as £50 a session (some of the more expensive aromatherapists or shiatsu therapists may charge this). But, all in all, the knowledge that you are receiving individual attention may make these therapies — and their price tags — worthwhile.

Alternative treatments can give new hope and incentives to get better; they can often help sufferers to cope better with their symptoms and more than occasionally they can achieve a cure. These therapies seem to represent the direction in which modern health is heading; perhaps they do hold a cure for you.

# 6

# AND ON TO THE NEXT GENERATION

'I don't want my children to grow up with my problems,' says many an agoraphobic or anxiety-ridden mother. Any kind of panic or anxiety state is difficult for a mother and for her family to cope with. Even if not housebound, there are problems with taking children to school, to the doctor, attending functions at school and many other incidences.

Of course, agoraphobia is only one problem. Even a mildly anxious parent may infect their children with their own fears by being over-protective and over-cautious. Unfortunately, these days children *have* to be alerted to many dangers but it is the everyday, seemingly harmless remarks that reveal the underlying anxieties of the mother and signal to the child that life is fraught with danger.

'Eat your food or you will be ill'; 'Be careful, you'll hurt yourself'; 'A stranger means danger'; 'Don't touch that dog'. The list goes on.

In themselves, the cautionary remarks are perfectly reasonable and realistic; it is the attitude of the parent that may convey excessive worry. The child must be warned against trying to hug a strange dog, but how often do we see a mother swooping on her child – often with a smack – snatching it away from the dog and scolding wildly, 'Bad dog . . . he'll bite you'. This over-reaction will go well on the way to ensuring that the child will develop a fear and perhaps later, a phobia of dogs.

My own mother was very nervous and almost housebound with agoraphobia for two years when my brother and I were young. She was particularly sensitive to loud noises and sudden shocks and we learned early that we shouldn't yell at each other or bang doors. To shout 'Mummy, come quick!' provoked a violent over-reaction as she always expected the worst. It was inevitable that one of us at least would develop similar anxieties. Me.

All babies are born with an in-built fear response to sudden noises, heights and anything unfamiliar or unusual but some children have a more sensitive, anxious temperament than others. Opinion is divided as to whether this is hereditary. Physiological imbalances causing reactions to situations *can* be inherited. This was accepted by the American Psychiatric Association in 1988 who concluded that a panic attack is a biological condition that runs in families and could even be manifest in childhood. Apart from an in-built predisposition to panic, anxiety is infectious and can easily be passed from nervous mother to edgy child and back again until both are thoroughly tense and upset.

By about eight months most children will display a fear of strangers and become distressed when separated from their mother. By two years old, infants will be starting to cope with these anxieties and to enjoy the beginnings of a social life.

As life becomes more interesting, children may also find new experiences that are upsetting. Fears of certain animals, darkness and thunderstorms are the usual problems, but a child usually grows out of these by the time he is around six years old. If a parent (or parents) has fears that have persisted into adulthood, his or her child may well have the same trouble as it gets older. Parents really do have a responsibility to help their children to face up to their fears and gradually overcome them. Unfortunately, the adult's phobias may be so deeply entrenched that they are so engrossed with trying to cope with their own fears they don't realize the damage they are doing to the child. The child may well begin to copy the way his parent reacts in certain situations and develop the same avoidance behaviour. This copying is called modelling. It is not surprising then that a child, seeing its parent display fear of certain things may well learn to fear those things too. In this way a phobia passes from adult to child. For instance, if a child's mother shrieks at the sight of a spider, it is likely that that child will also develop a fear of spiders, based on nothing but his knowledge of his mother's fear.

Imagination can be a scary thing. As our minds develop and we learn to think, this can get out of control. We think of things we do not understand. Thoughts, dreams and fantasies can get mixed up together and although these can sometimes be pleasurable, for a very imaginative, highly-strung child they can be very frightening. And what frightens a child can change from one day to the next.

Adults are often likely to make mistakes about the things that upset children. A visit to a circus or pantomime can set up a fear for life of clowns or characters that are not quite human. It is amazing how many two year olds are carried screaming from a theatre or circus ring and suffer from nightmares for months afterwards. Many adults still carry a dislike of theatrical characters and remember the occasion when they were terrified originally.

Pure fantasy is less frightening to a child, however shocking, than real life and fantasy becoming intermingled. My daughter at five years old was not a nervous child but she became hysterical on one occasion when watching a television programme about a little girl cartoon character who wished that her hair would grow. Her hair became longer and longer until it spread out of the house and down the garden – and Busy Lizzie couldn't stop the wish. It was the 'out-of-control' situation that upset Alyson, and, to her five-year-old mind, it was something that could quite conceivably happen to her.

In the last century, a child psychiatrist named Heinrich Hoffmann wrote a series of verses to amuse his young patients. Entitled *Struwwelpeter*, this book has alternately entertained and terrified generations of children since. What effect the verses had on the patients themselves has not been recorded. The stories were about unusual characters: there was the hyperactive fidgety Phil, who couldn't sit still; anorexic Augustus, a chubby lad who came to a sad end when he wasted away:

> But one day, one cold winter's day
> He screamed out, 'Take the soup away!

Oh take the nasty soup away!
I won't have any soup today.'

As for poor little 'Suck-a-Thumb' who lost his fingers to the 'great, long, red-legged scissor-man', he must have given many Victorian children nightmares. My grandfather insisted that his elder sister's phobia of scissors and knives stemmed from her childhood horror of that book.

On the whole, however, perhaps the 'toughening-up' that the Victorian and Edwardian young experienced at an early age actually helped them to face up to fear and prevented the development of serious phobias in later life.

These examples indicate how insensitive to a child's imagination and fears adults can be. Of course, the majority of children do not grow up to be phobic; in fact, a certain amount of stress does little harm and teaches them to cope with their feelings — unpleasant memories causing no more than a shudder. We have no way of knowing how many young people suffered from phobias and anxiety states in years gone by. It was likely that such fears were hidden under a blanket of general ill health, and for girls particularly, to be hyper-sensitive was often looked upon as an admirable feminine trait.

Today, many middle-aged people can trace the onset of their anxiety state to a traumatic incident in their childhood when they had to be hospitalized and separated from their mother and/or father, sometimes for a period of weeks. In addition, they may have had an operation and been subjected to the anaesthetics of the day, which were applied through a rubber mask.

It is accepted that lasting emotional damage can be done to children in these circumstances and hospitals today go to great lengths to ensure that children understand and accept medical procedures with the least distress. Most important of all, they ensure that the younger ones are not separated from their parents. In the Open Door and PAX records are many descriptions of a first panic attack occurring in childhood after a hospital experience.

In the late Thirties everyone was expected to practise wearing gas masks because of the impending war. Associating these with the hospital anaesthetic masks, the rubbery smell and the slightly unreal, out-of-focus view of the world was enough to re-awaken unpleasant memories of hospital and panic. This was one of those occasions when fear had to be faced and overcome. Teachers and parents conducted their own form of exposure therapy, gradually acclimatizing the children to wearing their gas masks.

The world is a frightening place to the imaginative child who is beginning to question why he is here, and trying to tackle the formidable subjects of life and death. As always, it is the 'great unknown' that is most frightening. Behind a fear of death, for instance, is the feeling of deep-rooted fear and insecurity, of being parted forever from parents or loved ones. The fact that many parents cannot or will not talk about death adds to the anxiety about it, an anxiety that can build up over the years to phobic proportions.

In earlier times death was discussed openly; today it has become a taboo subject. Brothers and sisters often died young and even parents sometimes died in their prime; but though it was distressing, it was accepted that death was part of life. After all, everyone knew that dead people went to Heaven and one had the comforting assurance of the Church that one's loved ones had joined the company of angels.

These days, because children and many adults have never had to deal with a death in the family or among friends, it is rarely mentioned. If a death does occur in the family both child and adult need professional counselling to help them through bereavement. Death phobias *do* occur in young children, though you will rarely come across this subject discussed in books or articles about childhood fears. Because death is intangible, something children tend to fear more than physical things, even adult explanations can not always serve to reduce the fear . . . particularly since many contemporary adults feel the same way themselves.

From the age of ten onwards, I never went to bed without worrying about whether I would wake up the next morning. The situation became so bad that I would read through the night and even when I did drop off to sleep I would leave the light on. 'Could death creep up and take over from sleep?' I asked my parents. After all, they had taught me to pray 'If I should die before I wake I pray The Lord my soul to take.'

'Don't be morbid,' they said, and the subject was dropped. Unknowingly, it was their avoidance of the issue that made it all the more frightening. After all, if my parents couldn't discuss it, there must be some reason why it was unmentionable.

'They'll grow out of it,' say adults when referring to childhood fears; and, of course, the majority of children do shed their fears in due course. But there are always those who are generally more highly strung and nervous, who accumulate fears from childhood onwards which may provide the basis for a full-fledged anxiety state in later life.

Very young children quickly learn to cope with feelings of mild anxiety. Rocking, thumb-sucking, a comfort blanket or teddy bear or even a special piece of rag helps them to feel relaxed. These things are called *soteria*, a term for an object or situation from which children (and adults, too, as we shall see later) derive disproportionate comfort. Teddy bears are good examples of soteria, providing comfort and reassurance to youngsters who take them to bed throughout childhood and beyond, often never parting with them at all.

Later on, between the ages of five and ten, most children develop rituals – repeated actions that have a special meaning for the performer. Rituals bring a sense of comfort and are used as a way of reducing anxiety. At this age they are not a problem, but in an over-anxious adult all manner of protective rituals may be built up, which, although they control anxiety to an extent, can themselves become a serious problem.

Over-protective parents are likely to have over-anxious children because the adult's worries are easily transmitted to the child, who gets little opportunity to face up to and cope with a feared situation. Parents pass on feelings of fear to their children when they communicate their own exaggerated anxieties and gradually the children perceive the world through their parents' eyes as a threatening place.

PAX members were asked to write about their childhood

anxieties and about their parents' attitudes. More important, they were asked if they could link their present anxieties and phobias to their early upbringing. Although many people felt that they had not been influenced by their parents, others said they could relate their phobias to their parents' (usually mothers') over-reactions to childhood behaviour. Here are some examples:

If I came home from school half an hour late my mother would be in a state of near-hysteria. I soon learned that I had to keep her informed of my every movement, telephone home every so often to tell her what I was doing and how long I would be. By the time I was grown up I felt I had to continue maintaining close contact – not for my mother's sake, but for mine, as by now *I* was nervous when I was not in touch with home.

I longed to have a bicycle but mother said they were dangerous, that I might fall off and break a limb or damage my face and need plastic surgery. I occasionally borrowed friends' bikes but I didn't enjoy riding them as my imagination would race ahead and I would visualize myself being rushed to hospital in an ambulance.

If a mother is constantly warning her child to be careful she is saying there is danger. It is sometimes difficult to judge the line between reasonable caution and excessive worrying. These days, I can see certain aspects of life through my own mother's eyes and smile at her lifelong anxieties. I can tease her about them, too. I know that when I say I am making a certain journey, which I do regularly and which involves crossing the Severn Bridge, she visualizes this as something like a rope bridge slung across a ravine in the jungle. She would deny this, of course, but that's the way her mind works. We have a ritual when I telephone her from the car and I say, 'We've just reached the middle of the bridge.'

'Well hurry and get off it,' she replies . . . and she means it!

If one is subjected to constant parental warnings during one's formative years, these will come to represent the basic attitude towards life and one's inclination to behave in certain ways. The anxious person must learn to discard all the dire warnings she has been subjected to all her life and learn to be unafraid by facing up to and banishing her childhood fears.

As we can see from the next chapter, a phobic childhood can be even more frightening than phobias in adulthood. It's important to banish those fears in our children, before what should be the most worry-free period of their lives is destroyed.

# 7

# ON A PERSONAL NOTE

My own story is a classic example of how fears can develop in a highly strung child, paving the way for panic attacks and multiple phobias. My mother was severely agoraphobic for two years and was virtually housebound. Because I had a nanny, my life was carefully structured and over-protected, and for my first few years, with grandmothers and a couple of aunts around, I was the centre of the family's attention. When my brother came along some of the attention was diverted. You will note that my father, like most fathers of the time, was very much on the periphery.

I had a governess until I was nearly seven, after which school, though enjoyable, was a bit of a shock to the system. Around the time I started school, it was thought necessary for me to have my tonsils removed. I spent two weeks in hospital in a ward with eight elderly ladies who, I was convinced, were all on the point of death. I had never been in contact with anyone who was ill before, and I hated the idea of being one of these sick people.

The operation was the most terrifying thing that had ever happened to me. I was held down on the operating table, kicking and screaming and being scolded while the anaesthetic mask was held down over my face. I still look back on this as one of the worst experiences of my life. The feeling of losing conscious ness was the same unreal sensation which would dominate the anxiety attacks I was to experience later, and for years I was sure I could actually smell the anaesthetic gas.

A few weeks later, the stay in hospital just a bad dream, I was enjoying my weekly dancing class when someone switched on a light and I was immediately engulfed in what I could only describe to the adults present as a 'funny feeling'. It was not panic, but rather a nightmare sensation of unreality and I was bewildered rather than frightened. The grown-ups decided that I was suffering from a nervous reaction to the recent operation and I was kept away from school for several weeks.

I never went back to that dancing class, but a few weeks later the 'funny feeling' hit me in school assembly and I ran out of the hall to escape from the sensation. And later, even when I was having fun at a party during a game of Blind Man's Buff, the unreal feeling – as though everything was happening to someone else – struck again.

'An anxiety attack,' said the doctor.

'It's only nerves,' said my mother but I felt unwell for several days.

During the summer holidays, we went to stay in the country where I rode my pony and, with my friend, went for rides through the fields and woods which took us miles away from home. One morning we went to pick raspberries. It was a baking hot summer day and all at once I began to feel unreal, hot and muzzy. I ran all the way home and stayed indoors for the rest of the day. When it happened a couple more times I began to get really alarmed, but the grown-ups kept blaming it on nerves, so I stopped talking about it.

I moved to a new school in the autumn and to my relief the anxiety attacks stopped. I was good at my school work and enjoyed being with the other girls. The only thing I hated was PE, always worrying about being blind-folded for indoor games or having to practise handstands or hanging upside-down on wallbars, because I hated the sensation and felt dizzy and disoriented. Although I was an athletic girl I soon learned to be clumsy so that I could avoid having to do certain exercises. Swimming was another activity I hated as I had no confidence in the water. By rubbing soap in my eyes I convinced my teachers that I was allergic to some chemical in the swimming pool.

I was free of anxiety attacks for over a year and had almost forgotten what they were like when they suddenly returned and really got a hold. Morning assembly at school became an ordeal which had to be faced every day, but the dread of it remained with me every waking moment. Most nights were disturbed by troubled dreams and at breakfast I would feel sick and tearful, filled with dread about the coming day. The journey to school involved a long walk, a bus ride and another walk. This itself was becoming more and more difficult as panic was always just below the surface, waiting to strike if I allowed myself to stop and think. I became addicted to day-dreaming to get away from the situation, pretending to be another more glamorous person triumphing over difficult and heroic situations. In my fantasy life *I* was in control.

When filing into the school hall for assembly my first thought was always what the hymn for the day was and how many verses it ran to. Up to three was bearable, but any more and the panic would well up, making me feel sick, dizzy and unsteady. My great dread was that I might faint, though I never did. As things got worse I frequently had to slip out of the hall with the excuse that I felt 'unwell'. There was no point in trying to explain further, I'd tried that and nobody understood.

Then sitting through lessons became difficult and I was trying to avoid assembly as often as possible by being late for school. The atmosphere which I had once enjoyed was becoming unbearable. Too many people, too much noise, my mind felt over-loaded and I could not concentrate on my lessons. I withdrew from my friends who found me 'odd'. I still managed to hang on, though too many days off meant my school work was affected.

Boarding school, my parents decided, and I went along with this idea. A new start, a different atmosphere, new friends. I had read so many books about girls' boarding schools and I knew it was all going to be jolly good fun . . . midnight feasts, new friends and lots of practical jokes. Above all there would be no travelling to school. The daily journey to my present school was becoming a nightmare in itself. Being privately coached soon helped me to regain my educational level and my confidence was returning when I passed the entrance exam to the new school.

It took about a term for the novelty to wear off. The feelings of anxiety which had been pushed below the surface began to trouble me once more and I felt increasingly trapped. Sleeping in a dormitory with rigid rules about not talking after lights-out and no reading in bed left me with too much time alone with my thoughts and my out-of-control imagination. Meal times meant more rules and there were no acceptable excuses to leave the table. Eating became a problem with so many others watching and noticing any jittery behaviour.

At first, I was able to cope with services in the school chapel (twice each day and three times on Sunday) but inevitably as the panicky feelings began to recur I found it more and more difficult to sit still until the end of a service. Lessons were becoming an ordeal, too. I would clock watch. Twenty minutes till the bell goes . . . ten minutes . . . five minutes. Little wonder that I started to slip behind with my school work again. Sitting through a forty-minute lesson period was purgatory. The feeling of being trapped increased even when I was sitting near a door. There was, of course, no chance of asking to be excused. You might get away with it on one occasion . . . if you could plead an emergency . . . but not a second time.

I asked my parents to take me away and let me return to the local high school. Panic attacks and daily assembly would be preferable to a twenty-four-hour school environment. I said I was unhappy at boarding school and told some lurid stories about life in that eminently respectable establishment. Being unhappy was reason enough where my sensible parents were concerned but I was grilled by headmistress, house mistress and other members of the staff, who insisted on being told why I wanted to leave their precious school.

Was I leaving because I was so unpopular? I was indignant about that theory as I had many friends. Anything wrong at home? Death in the family? Bankruptcy? I looked at them blankly and then explained that I suffered from delayed shell shock after my – mostly imaginary – experiences during the Blitz. Did they believe me? I never found out.

It was so good to make another fresh start at my former school that I felt practically normal again. It didn't last, of course, but as the old feelings came creeping back the time had come to do something about the problem. Hauled up for the ninth time before the headmistress I found that at the age of fifteen I could at last explain *why* I was invariably late for school. I never had to sit through morning assembly again. I was allowed to slip into one of the side rooms if I felt unwell. Better still, I was not forced to attend at all but could wait in the classroom until the others returned. My form teacher let me sit near the door and I had permission to slip outside the class for a few moments if tensions built up.

Once I started to explain, I found that I could talk about the things that bothered me and arrange to tackle problems such as hanging upside-down or standing on my head in PE. I would take a packed lunch instead of eating with the crowd – but that didn't last long as I found I was missing out on most of the gossip, so I was soon back lunching with my friends. The best thing was that no one thought there was anything peculiar about me. Looking back, I feel that it was strange that at no time did anyone feel there was any reason for me to see a doctor!

I scrambled through my exams. There were too many gaps in my education for me to do really well. At last I reached my last days at school . . . I didn't want to leave!

I was not to know that I would not be free of anxieties and panic attacks until I was in my late twenties. There were periods of remission when I hoped that the problem had gone for good, though during these times I was still very anxiety-prone and had built up an extraordinary collection of various phobias. Perhaps 'phobia' in these cases is too strong a word – after all, a fear only becomes a phobia when it prevents the sufferer from leading a normal life. And, as a child who suffers from a physical disability has to learn to cope with it, so I managed to live with my fears.

I did go out of my way to avoid all the things that upset me. These included such things as balloons, skeletons, people with any deformity, hospitals, dentists' and doctors' surgeries, being blindfolded, hanging upside-down, travelling any distance, sleeping away from home, nose-bleeds, abstract thoughts, infinity, cemeteries, clouds, darkness, silence – the list was almost endless. There seemed to be so many upsetting things to cope with and I was only really happy in the fantasy world into which I slipped at every available opportunity.

When I was eighteen, I felt that it was time to face up to my fears and learn to overcome them gradually. Life became much rosier, I did not need my day-dreams so much and I began to feel like a normal person for the first time. The fears were fading and soon I had a job and a full social life.

Then, just after my twenty-first birthday, I had 'flu. Feeling a bit under par, I was waiting at a bus stop in the centre of London when the full range of half-forgotten sensations flooded over me. It had been so long since I had experienced the feelings of unreality and panic that I had forgotten how dreadful they were; I could not handle them and had to get a taxi home, where it took me the rest of the day to recover my equilibrium. I took a whole week off work, reasoning that I had not completely recovered from the 'flu and that the old symptoms had returned because of my poor state of health. However, the following Monday when I arrived at the same bus stop . . . back came the feelings of panic.

Every day from then on was a continual fight against rising panic and feelings of unreality. I had to reach the centre of London each day and every morning I felt sick with apprehension in anticipation of the journey. I was determined to hide my distress; I could not bear anyone to know about it and had a dread of making a fool of myself in front of other people, so I was determined not to draw attention to myself though I may have looked somewhat twitchy and uncomfortable to anyone who studied me carefully as I stood at the bus stop. I carried a piece of paper on which I had written my name, address, date and destination. When the real world started to slide and my memory played tricks, I would read this over and over again to reassure myself that I really existed.

I loved my job and dreaded the fact that I might have to give it up despite the misery of getting to the office each day. Sometimes when I felt really bad, I would think of looking for work nearer home, but I knew instinctively that once I gave in, the agoraphobia symptoms would follow me: then I would give up the local job and retreat into my home. I had to conquer the problem before it conquered me.

I combed libraries and bookshops looking for information about agoraphobia and panic, but at that time there was very little written for the lay person and what I could find frightened me even more. I went to see a psychiatrist. 'You are probably really quite a nice young woman,' he told me! 'But you are obsessed with your symptoms which are caused by an anxiety state, and you will just have to learn to overcome them.' I had hoped that some sort of treatment might be available, but was warned off by the great man who felt that as I did not appear to have any underlying problems and was managing to cope – just – any treatment might result in aggravating the condition rather than curing it.

No treatment, just keep going! At least I had acquired one comforting piece of information: agoraphobia would not kill me and it would not ruin my life unless I let it. I am afraid there is no spectacular recovery to report – just several more years of working through it, learning to relax and not be afraid of myself. It took me some time to realize that it was not the dreaded situations themselves which were the problem, but my own reactions to them.

Gradually it all faded; I hardly realized how much I was progressing until it became obvious that my nerves were no longer dominating my life. It takes some time to appreciate that one is really free. The biggest bonus was discovering that all the other anxieties also disappeared, until instead of being a permanently anxious person with many devastating fears, I discovered that I had become less fearful than most of the people I knew; that having trained myself not to worry, *I did not worry*.

But *how* do you work through phobias, *how* do you conquer them? In later chapters we will look at some of the techniques you can try to help you overcome your fears.

There are a number of childhood and adolescent fears and phobias which you or your children may have suffered from.

Some of these go on to have an effect on adult life, but they won't if you don't let them. Understanding them is the key.

## SCHOOL PHOBIA

Many experts feel this is not a true phobia, that children are normally not avoiding school as such but are trying to avoid separation from home and parents. Others are of the opinion that children are more afraid of the school than of leaving their mothers. Some are afraid both of school and of separation from their parents.

### What are They Frightened of at School?

Many very young children are understandably nervous when starting school, finding the general bustle overwhelming and having to adjust to working and playing in close proximity to large numbers of other children. Of course, the majority quickly settle down. Unfortunately, where there are problems it often becomes the mother or father's problem rather than the child's. He or she may keep the child at home, hoping that next day he will feel more able to face the ordeal of school, that the tummy aches, sore throats and temperatures will disappear and he will go off quite happily.

It doesn't happen like this, of course. As soon as avoidance techniques are used, the return to school will be more and more difficult – for the parent as well as for the child.

Many studies have shown that most young children who are nervous at school are over-dependent on their parents – usually the mother – but that this over-dependence has been largely fostered by the parents themselves. In 1958, a study of twenty-six children (*Eisenberg, Baltimore*) showed that the mothers were found to be more anxious than usual and had been able to communicate to the children their own anxious attitude to life.

PAX receives a number of letters from mothers of children who are distressed at the thought of going to school, particularly at the beginning of a school year when their child first goes to 'proper' school. 'My little boy of six is school phobic,' wrote one mother. 'After two weeks at school he is very distressed and says he will never go back.' In fact, with the help of a sympathetic head teacher he was back at school within a fortnight and had settled down completely by the middle of term.

The term 'school phobic' is tossed around too lightly today, frequently being used to describe a fear that though upsetting is perfectly rational. Fear of bullies, fear of making a silly mistake and being laughed at by classmates or being told off by a teacher. The true school phobic child can not explain what it is that he is afraid of. They may offer various 'reasonable' excuses when pressed by adults because they cannot describe what it is that really upsets them. My parents could not understand why I found it impossible to explain how I felt. I *knew* it was my feelings and my reactions to certain situations which were upsetting me and it is very difficult for a child to understand itself, never mind trying to explain to adults.

No, I was not frightened of anything in particular, but a pack of noisy children on the move could seem overwhelming to one who preferred to stay quietly in one place. There was a desperate need to escape – from the other children; the frightening surge of the crowd when a bell sounded; the over-powering sense of being trapped in the assembly hall; the feeling of tension which could build up in a lesson when you were stuck at a desk in the classroom, unable to break the tension by slipping out of the room for a few moments.

The extrovert child will get rid of its energy in the playground, on the sports field, or in the gymnasium, but the quieter one may be left with a lot of bottled-up tension and no way of working it off. Disliking to be naughty or noisy in class, he or she can find the tension unbearable; trying to concentrate on the lesson may be impossible. The instinct is then to break away from the pack of children, the discipline of the classroom, the ordeal of assembly. Because it is not possible to escape, the obvious thing is to try to avoid these situations in future.

School phobias affect to some degree about two or three children in every hundred, usually manifesting themselves when there is a change of school at eleven years old. The impact of a very large school on a nervous child can be over-powering, a fact which many adults do not seem to appreciate. In severe cases, the build-up of anxiety can result in panic attacks – usually in assembly or when tension becomes unbearable. Dread of a recurrence of these attacks causes the child to avoid the situations where they occurred. This can lead to an avoidance of school altogether because the panic attacks increase to include the journey to school. This becomes a classic agoraphobia with panic attacks occurring anywhere away from home.

It is important that the phobic child is treated at this stage. An adolescent agoraphobe is in a sorry plight, particularly if she becomes housebound. Lack of contact with other teenagers may result in a teenager retreating into day-dreams and fantasies – living life through books and television and avoiding contact with the real world outside the home. It is particularly difficult to persuade adolescents to take part in any treatment programme, as recovery means having to face up to the problems of normal everyday life.

If school phobia is latent agoraphobia, in many cases it *can* be treated with exposure therapy techniques. It is felt more and more that such children would be happier being taught at home, or even better in small groups with others who cannot tolerate school. Personally, I am very undecided about the benefit of this in the long run. Certainly, as a child I would have jumped at the chance of opting out of 'ordinary' school. I would have felt more relaxed and would probably have done better in lessons and exams. Oh the relief of not having to travel to school and face the daily torments! But it is like putting sticky plaster on a broken leg. The injury has to be dealt with, the bone set and then a long period of physiotherapy ensures that the bone won't collapse when it is walked on.

If I hadn't learnt to face up to anxiety and panic attacks in school I would have found it even more difficult when experiencing the extra stresses of growing up and facing the outside world with agoraphobic tendencies still present and unresolved. Children of agoraphobic mothers are more prone to school phobia and may develop agoraphobic tendencies in later life.

In 1976 Berg surveyed 786 women with agoraphobia, 299

of whom were married and had at least one child aged between seven and fifteen years. He showed that school phobia occurred to a greater extent in their children than would be expected. (Fourteen per cent in the eleven to fifteen year old age group.) Also, those agoraphobic mothers whose children developed school phobia had had the disorder themselves to some extent.

A further finding was that a history of school phobia in these agoraphobic women was associated with an earlier onset of subsequent agoraphobia in adulthood with more severe symptoms. Though a formal survey was never undertaken, the phobia histories of four thousand Open Door members were studied in 1970 and it was found that twenty per cent of these women had suffered from school phobia to some degree.

## Suggestions for Tackling School Phobia

Here is a brief parents' guide to helping your child get over a real or imagined school phobia, and preventing one from happening.

1. Parents should study their own behaviour, trying to assess how it might be affecting their child and making an effort to modify it. For example, avoid telling horror stories of your own schooldays, or even making school an issue. Don't express shock or fear when your child relates a school 'trauma'. Be matter of fact and mildly sympathetic. Avoid over-reacting.

2. Young children who are showing signs of anxiety and stress and having learning difficulties should be screened for physical problems such as:
- inner-ear dysfunction, which might cause balance problems;
- perception defects which could result in dyslexia;
- infantile reflexes which might indicate some degree of neuro-developmental delay (see Chapter 3).

Physiological troubles may be the cause of your child's panic or fear. Don't assume it's psychological.

3. If a child is behaving in a bizarre fashion – for instance, putting all his shoes in the dustbin, hiding in a cupboard, or retreating into a 'safe' fantasy world, consult your doctor and the school, asking to be referred to a psychologist who is *au*

*fait* with school phobia. Don't frighten your child by drawing undue attention to his unusual behaviour. Again, don't over-react.

4. If your child is trying to avoid school, the obvious thing is to ask what is wrong. If there is a specific problem that can be solved — worry about schoolwork, bullying — you will obviously work out the solution with the teachers. Speak to your child casually about his worries, not demanding an answer to your questions, or forcing him to be forthcoming. Show a genuine interest but don't appear over-anxious.

5. When the answer is 'I don't know what is wrong', you will have to work through the events of a normal school day to try and pinpoint the root of your child's fear. Can it lie perhaps in:

- Leaving home and the journey to school? However inconvenient, the child should be escorted to ensure he/she actually reaches school. He might just need a 'kick start' to get him out of the home, settling down normally when he reaches school.

- Morning assembly? This is a major problem with phobic children in the older age group. It can inspire feelings of claustrophobia, having to stand or sit in the centre of a crowd of children with no possibility of leaving without becoming the centre of attention. If the school can be persuaded to recognize that this is a problem, it is possible that some arrangements can be made for him to stay in the classroom, at the end of a line, at the back of the hall. Don't, however, force him to stand out in the crowd. Any arrangements should be made discreetly and your child should never feel he is abnormal, or treated specially. Make it clear he can return to the crowd as and when he pleases.

- Lunch time? A fear of eating in public is very common and can persist later in life. Of course it is hoped that a young person with this hang-up can eventually be helped to eat in company with his classmates, but initially it might be helpful to let him have a packed lunch each day. Try inviting his friends round for lunch a few times at the weekend. Perhaps exposure therapy . . . a little at a time . . . will do the trick.

- In the gymnasium? The PE teacher should allow the child to take part only in the exercises he feels happy about. Problems with balance and dizziness are often behind a fear of physical exercise, and having to hang upside-down, for instance, can accentuate these. Let him know these feelings are normal, and perhaps spend some time practising some of the more frightening feats at home. Let him know dizziness is a natural reaction, and that panic does not have to follow.
- In the classroom? Another place in which to feel trapped. It should be possible for the child to be allowed to sit near the door so that he can slip out if the tension builds up. A few minutes to calm down can prevent a panic attack developing. This has proved a very successful move in many cases. Again, don't draw attention to the problem among his classmates. Give him the tools, a helping hand and a sympathetic ear, but he must sort it out for himself. As soon as he realizes there really is nothing to fear, you'll find that special measures are unnecessary.

These are some very basic steps to help a child to control feelings of anxiety and hopefully to avoid panic attacks. *Of course* it is often not nearly as simple as this and there should be no delay in seeking specialist help with the problem instead of trying to force the child to school without adult understanding and guidance. But, on the other hand, your over-reaction could exacerbate the problem. There is a fine line between help and hindrance – keep an eye out for it.

However helpful the staff at school might be there is always the problem of the other children – they may not be so understanding if they feel someone is 'different'! They *may* cooperate if asked to help their classmate through a difficult time but it might be preferable to refer vaguely to 'breathless attacks' or 'dizzy spells' rather than 'nerves' or 'panic'. Better still, if the staff can implement the necessary changes without drawing attention to your child, he'll feel much more comfortable.

Britain's leading specialist on phobias, Professor Isaac Marks says, 'Whatever the cause of school phobia, prolonged absence can lead to serious consequences which may be lifelong. The child loses touch with friends, social skills wither and education suffers. The habit of avoiding unpleasantness may grow, so that in later years that person will cope more poorly with the slings and arrows of outrageous fortune with which we all must learn to contend.'

School phobias can be averted if tackled in the early stages by parents and teachers, together with professional help if necessary.

# 8

# CONTROLLING THE FEAR

In further chapters we will look at many different fears and phobias and examine the ways in which you can do something to help yourself to overcome them. But before tackling *any* phobias you must prepare yourself physically and emotionally by learning to control your inner anxieties.

## *BREATHING*

Most anxious people don't realize that they are breathing wrongly and that this is an actual *cause* of feelings of anxiety. If you attended one of the major stress management courses you would find that the first thing they concentrate on is the way in which you breathe.

When a wild animal scents danger, for a second or so it freezes in its tracks and stays perfectly still, wide-eyed and alert, holding its breath as though any sound of breathing will affect its concentration. Then the tension suddenly snaps and the creature leaps in the direction of safety.

We may catch our breath if we have a narrow escape; in a dangerous situation we behave like the animal, for fear is experienced and the reaction is immediate. Holding our breath is a normal response when we are suddenly surprised or in some kind of danger – a response which is usually corrected automatically as we gasp with relief and inhale, deeply filling our lungs with air.

But for the chronically anxious person this does not always happen – her nervous system has been conditioned to react to dangers that exist only in her mind, and her body responds by remaining constantly on the alert, with muscles tense and breathing fast and shallow.

The average person reacts to excitement by increasing the rate and amplitude of his or her breathing; the chronically anxious person, on the other hand, attempts to control her emotions by interfering with her breathing, deliberately trying to appear calm and controlled and hiding her natural urge to pant and gasp as she takes shallow breaths and blocks off her oxygen supply. During a panic attack she may fold her arms or clasp her hands across her diaphragm – literally 'pulling herself together' – as she struggles for control. This posture accentuates the automatic constriction of the chest when it is deprived of oxygen. The sufferer can not exhale and inhale properly; in other words, she simply cannot breathe correctly, and she is not aware of what she is doing as she tenses all the wrong muscles in a desperate attempt to appear normal.

No gasp, sob or cry for help will pass her lips if she can possibly help it. How dreadful it would be to expose one's weakness and emotions, she thinks. Someone without anxiety problems, without the same need to display a brave front in a dodgy situation will allow herself to let out a yell of fright and her breathing will quickly return to normal when the cause of fear has disappeared.

Everyone knows that the body needs oxygen in order to stay alive but the rate and depth of breathing controlled by the respiratory centre in the brain is affected not by a lack of oxygen but by the concentration of carbon dioxide in the blood. If we over-breathe and take in more air than our body needs, too much carbon dioxide is 'washed' out of the blood resulting in dizziness, tingling in the fingers and other unpleasant sensations.

Hyperventilation is the term used to describe over-breathing and many people breathe too rapidly or too deeply for their body's requirements. In this case, your short rapid breaths do not allow proper exhalation of carbon dioxide from your lungs, which again leads to dizziness and often nausea. Learning to breathe correctly – that is, at a suitable rate using the diaphragm rather than the chest – can make dramatic changes to how you feel.

Anxiety is greatly increased if the breathing pattern is incorrect and just altering this pattern can change someone from a nervous wreck to a competent, relaxed person. To check if you are breathing correctly, stand up and place one hand on your chest and the other on your abdomen. Breathe normally and check which hand is moving. If your lower hand is moving and the hand on your upper chest is still, you are using your diaphragm and breathing correctly from the bottom of your lungs.

Place your hands together on the top of your abdomen with the middle fingers touching, and try to 'breathe them apart'. If you practise doing this it will ensure that you are breathing properly from the bottom of your lungs.

It is important to practise breathing correctly *every day*, several times a day, until it becomes automatic. *It is absolutely no good* thinking about this when you are in the middle of a panic attack because by then you have lost control of your breathing. Concentrating on your breathing *before* the attack takes place will lighten its effects and in many cases prevent it from happening altogether.

## Emergency Measures

If you've lost control of your breathing when an attack hits there is the first aid trick with a paper bag to fall back on. It sounds silly until you appreciate exactly what you are doing. If you exhale into a paper bag and breathe back the same air, you are correcting the balance by re-breathing the carbon dioxide you have lost. More importantly, however, you are regulating your breathing, forcing yourself to slow down. After doing this several times the panic starts to subside. *It does work*. I am assured that a plastic bag is equally as good as a paper one (as long as you don't put it right over your head!) Also, several people have told me that they have perfected the technique of breathing into their cupped hands. If you can do this you wouldn't be so conscious of making an exhibition of yourself in public . . . nor would you have to remember always to carry a bag around with you.

115

Much better, however, to practise your breathing regularly.

# RELAXATION

Nervous anxiety, unlike fear and normal vigilance, has no way of discharging itself which means that the nervous person continually spends energy trying to control the 'fight or flight' syndrome which forms part of her anxiety state. As a result, she is liable to suffer from tension states which derive as much from the need to control anxiety as they do from actually experiencing it.

Hundreds of years ago primitive man was constantly on the alert for danger. We do not have the same life-threatening situations to deal with today, but our body reacts in the same way to the stresses and strains of our particular lifestyle and especially to the over-sensitive signals from our brains, which are wrongly telling us that we are in danger.

When learning to relax, we help our bodies to replace the flight response with messages to loosen tensed muscles. By releasing tension you help to signal to the mind that your situation is not dangerous, that there is no need to run away. Most anxious people become tense at the very idea of relaxing because to them 'letting go' means abandoning control. Your first attempts at practising relaxation seriously may result in a heightened level of anxiety because you are not used to being without tension.

Many people believe that relaxation is a natural and automatic procedure, but those who are tense and nervous have forgotten how to relax and have to be taught a lost skill. It is important to understand that you are about to lose control of your body by actually learning *how* to control it. By shutting out all distractions, you will direct each part of your body to feel pleasantly comfortable and free from tension.

There are a number of methods of relaxation but all are variations of a basic technique. Relaxation for Living (see page 205 for address) produces excellent cassettes. This organization also runs local classes and a correspondence course in relaxation techniques. It is important when choosing a relaxation cassette to ensure that the voice of the instructor does not grate on your nerves! So many people have recordings, some of which are very good indeed (others just churn out the identical exercises which you can read in any book), but if you don't like the timbre of the voice or the accent, this will irritate and you won't be able to concentrate.

Being chronically anxious, it is easy to avoid thinking too much about your body, just as you may not like to look at your reflection in the mirror because confronting yourself makes you feel nervous. It is important that you become familiar with your body.

Anxiety sufferers are particularly prone to tension in the head. Think of that 'tight band' round your forehead that causes those tension headaches, blurred vision, buzzing in the ears and difficulty in swallowing. The following will help you focus on the parts of the body that become tense, and to help relax them, ensuring that a peaceful calm takes the place of any anxiety.

*Head and Face:* Sit comfortably and accept that you are in control of all the muscles you are moving. Wrinkle up your face, raise and lower your eyebrows, and turn up your nose. Frown as hard as you can and then let go, relishing the feeling of relief. Push your tongue hard against the roof of your mouth, screw up your eyes and then let go again. Go through this routine two or three times until you really appreciate the relief from tension each time you relax the muscles. That's all for your first session. Don't go on to the next stage until you feel quite happy and comfortable.

*Arms and Hands:* Clench your left fist and, as you tighten up, concentrate on the tension in your hand, fist and arm. As you relax those muscles, note how loose they feel when you release the tension. Repeat this with your right hand and arm and then with both together.

*Upper Arms:* Press your elbows down and inwards and repeat several times.

*Chest, Shoulders and Back:* Pull your shoulders upwards and shrug several times. Bend your elbows and tense the muscles of your arms, then relax as you straighten them. Tilt your head backwards. Arch your back upwards and forward, then hunch yourself up pulling your shoulders forward. Release, and shake your upper body gently.

*Tummy and Bottom:* Pull in your stomach as hard as possible then 'push' it outwards. Imagine someone is going to punch you in your middle. Tighten up your buttocks and clench them together. Release.

*Legs:* Stiffen your legs and straighten your knees. Clench the muscles of your calves, press your heels down and stiffen your feet, pointing them upwards. Release.

*Ankles, Feet and Toes:* Curl up your toes and press your feet down. (If you get cramp easily in your feet, only do this for three seconds at a time.) Hold for a few seconds and relax.

Concentrate on one set of muscles at a time and spend five minutes or so flexing and relaxing them. When you feel ready, work your way through all of the exercises, finishing by tensing all your muscles at the same time and then relaxing them.

By this time you should have become accustomed to 'letting go' without anxiety building up. You might experience certain odd sensations such as slight disorientation, a floating feeling, tingling in your extremities (fingers and toes) and sensations of warmth. Accept the feelings instead of being frightened by them because they prove that you are becoming able to relax effectively.

If you have had no previous experience of relaxation exercises and are very tense to start with you might experience muscle spasms, such as twitches, tics and jerks – the sort of feeling you might sometimes have when dropping off to sleep. Again, don't let these worry you; just remind yourself how well you are doing.

# AUTOGENIC TRAINING

Autogenic training is another technique to prevent anxiety, tension and stress, but this should really only be attempted with an experienced therapist to guide you. Professor Marks, however, describes a very much simplified example:

> In this technique the person is asked to visualize one part of his body, to hold the image of that part and then to relax it. As an example: Get a clear picture of your right hand, see the outline of the fingers, the colour of the skin and nails, the wrinkles on your knuckles. Now relax your right hand as you think about it, keying the image in your mind all the time. Now try to see your right forearm in your mind's eye . . . etc. It does not seem terribly important which mode of relaxation is used, provided the person feels comfortably relaxed both muscularly and mentally.

# CREATIVE VISUALIZATION

A vivid imagination can often be a curse; it is up to you to change its direction and to learn to control it so that it becomes a source of pleasure and inspiration. Creative visualization works by helping you to replace negative images with positive ones. However successful you are with your breathing exercises and relaxation practice you must accept that you are still going to feel anxiety and panic when in your phobic situations or faced with your phobic object.

The importance of creative visualization is not that you will feel no panic, but that you do not suffer through continually anticipating it.

Suppose you are an agoraphobia sufferer. Before you can face the situation you dread so much it is vital that you change your attitude towards it. How long might you have to spend in that situation when you actually have to face it? A few minutes? An hour perhaps? But how long do you spend thinking about it, dreading it, living through it in your mind? Days and nights and hours and hours, like sucking on an aching tooth. Never, never, you think, could you face such a terrible experience in reality . . . but by now your perception of the problem has become totally distorted.

REALITY IS NEVER AS BAD AS ANTICIPATION.

Your misery and discomfort are caused by your subconscious mind, which is incapable of distinguishing between a real or imagined experience. Everything your conscious mind tells you, your subconscious will believe and accept as fact. If you imagine you are ill you will feel ill; if you picture the places where your agoraphobia manifests itself, or think about the animal, or other phobic object that terrifies you, your subconscious mind will react and the message will go out to your body to do the same. Now here come the jelly legs, the over-breathing, the dizzy sensations and all the other manifestations of fear.

You cannot control your subconscious mind by willpower. Giving it instructions will not work, as it does not comprehend words, only pictures. Many people assume that will power will help them overcome their problems. When it doesn't, they blame themselves for lacking strength of character . . . but they are trying to open a door with the wrong key.

## How to Harness Your Imagination

Practise using your imagination by creating pictures in your mind; pleasant scenes perhaps, recalling the faces and personalities of people you know. See them, hear what they are saying, look at what they are wearing. The best place and time for such practice sessions is in bed before you drop off to sleep at night. As you settle down, shut your eyes so that you are more susceptible to your inner thoughts – usually the worrying ones. Train yourself to create positive images instead of letting your mind wander untethered through the jungle of anxious and vivid scenes.

## Positive Thinking

How do you feel about yourself? Make two lists of beliefs you have about yourself – one of negative feelings and one of positive ones. The negative views of yourself might cover several sheets of paper, while the positive list will contain only about three or four things.

Suppose, for instance, you are agoraphobic. You might write down, 'I cannot leave the house.' Now try to phrase the same feeling in a more positive way: 'When I am better I will be able to go out.' See how you can trick your mind? By continually thinking you are housebound you will *be* housebound. By thinking you are going to make an effort to do something about your problem you will succeed.

Let us try some more.

| *Negative* | *Positive* |
|---|---|
| I am too fat. | Other people can manage to lose weight, so can I. |
| Nobody loves me. | I will make a point of being pleasant to others. If they don't respond that's their problem. |
| Life is boring, I am boring. | I will try and be enthusiastic about just one thing a day. Instead of watching TV soaps I will watch a programme I can learn something from, whether it is cooking, exercises or breeding budgerigars. |
| I am unhappy. | I will smile at my reflection in the mirror and this will cheer me up! |

If you have a poor self-image you must work on changing this. Get your partner, children, or the rest of the family to tell you positive things about yourself. You may not believe them at first but persevere and try and respond to complimentary remarks by saying 'thank you' or words to that effect.

Here it comes: 'But my family are not like that'; 'No one is nice to me, nobody pays me compliments'; 'I don't *have* anyone', you might say. As I have said already, you will just have to get on with it on your own. But *don't* feel sorry for yourself. And you might be surprised by the number of supporters you really *do* have.

## Affirmations

An affirmation is a positive thought that you repeat to yourself. Using affirmations allows you to select quality thoughts and implant them into your subconscious so that you can feel better about yourself. The old favourite is, 'Every day in every way I am getting better and better.'

There are certain points to remember when using affirmations. Firstly . . . your mind will always move to what you think about. If you think in a negative way, such as 'I won't feel well if I go out' or 'I won't be able to help the children with their homework', you are obviously going to get a negative result. Your mind will keep moving you towards what you say you can't or don't want to do. Think of the people who spend all their time talking about what they don't want and wondering why they always get it.

In a book entitled *Being Happy!*, author Andrew Matthews writes:

> I recall some of my school teachers used to have my classmates and me writing lines like 'I won't talk in class' and 'I won't be late' and 'I won't throw things at the teacher'. Little did they realize that, structured in that negative vein, they were actually promoting misbehaviour. As I reflect on what used to happen in my classes I would have to concede that they did this very effectively!

The second point to remember is that affirmations are more effective when you say them out loud or write them down. This way you won't get side-tracked. You involve more of your physical senses when you speak or write so the effect is more powerful.

Thirdly, repetition is important. If for years you have been telling yourself 'I feel rotten' or 'Nothing ever goes right for me', it's going to take some time for your subconscious mind to accept your new attitude. We will see how positive affirmations work when we look at the ways to tackle specific phobias.

## SELF-HELP GROUPS

There is no denying that for most of us it is important to have someone to turn to for reassurance and encouragement. Anyone involved in one of the organizations for phobia sufferers will tell you the first reaction of a new member is 'Thank God someone knows how I feel'. It is such a relief to write it all down, to talk to another sufferer, and to read about the ways in which other phobic people cope. Often such people have suffered alone for years, not realizing how many others shared the same symptoms and not knowing that anything could be done to help them.

If you intend to make contact with one of these groups, check if it has the backing of doctors or psychiatrists. If they are therapeutic groups make sure that they are supervised by someone who is qualified. There are too many amateur psychologists and 'counsellers' around who think that they can help; this can be dangerous when such people start delving into background anxieties without knowing how to help the patient resolve any problem that may be unearthed.

If you are particularly impressionable and over sensitive, do not be persuaded into making contact with other sufferers who may want to discuss symptoms interminably, give adverse reports on treatments that they or others have tried and failed, and discourage you from embarking on similar treatment which might be suitable in your case. Especially, you need to avoid these people who have been agoraphobic or in an intense anxiety state with random and inexplicable panic attacks for more than five or six years and who have made little or no progress towards recovery. Unfortunately, there is no doubt that some sufferers have accepted their panic or agoraphobia as a way of life and are inclined to encourage others to do the same.

None of the self-help organizations want to be used as an emotional dustbin, but they all collect their quota of problem members who can quickly spread alarm and despondency throughout the rest. If you feel that you would like to help others who are in a worse position than yourself that is great, but if your own progress is being hindered by others who are endlessly drawing on your time and sympathy, back out quickly.

On the positive side, these groups can offer information and advice, and details of treatment and hospitals where it is available. Some are purely social gatherings but others have the backing of doctors and professional assistance in planning self-help programmes.

# 9

# THE NUTS AND BOLTS OF PHOBIAS

In many cases, phobias are simply perfectly rational fears that have been allowed to get out of hand. In other cases, as we see with nearly every kind of phobia, the sufferer externalizes her or his feelings of anxiety by projecting them on to a specific object or situation which itself becomes the problem. It is easier to avoid that object or situation than it is to try and rationalize the internal feelings that are so distressing and don't seem to make sense to the sufferer.

To a phobic person, controlling their fear means avoiding the object of that fear. But this does not work. If you are truly phobic – and *anyone* can develop a phobia – the problem can dominate your life. You worry about it all the time, wondering if and when you might come across *it*. Let's look at one example – snakes. The snake phobic will think and dream of snakes, avoid books in which there may be a picture of a snake, never watch wildlife programmes on the television, and, although in this country it is highly unlikely that anyone will encounter a live serpent, walks in the countryside are definitely out. *Thinking* about the creature will induce feelings of anxiety – shaking, sweating, hyperventilating – which may escalate into a panic attack. It is not surprising that the sufferer tries to put it out of her mind.

Once a phobia is established, and if nothing is done about it, the sufferer is stuck with it for life. It won't just go away on its own.

But it doesn't have to be that way. There are measures that can halt a phobia dead in its tracks – and you *can* help yourself.

# GRADUATED EXPOSURE

The subject is introduced to her phobic object a little at a time – learning to look at pictures of it, touching dummies or models, and progressing slowly to actually being able to confront and learn to tolerate the real thing.

But, before you get to this stage you must *think* about it! Until you can tolerate it in your mind – using the creative visualization techniques (see page 119) – you cannot go any further.

'I can't *bear* to think about it,' people tell me, but this is avoiding the problem from the word go. You must visualize the object of your phobia, in this case a snake, in a harmless situation – say coiled up asleep under a tree in an idyllic spot. All right, so you hate that picture, but if you can face it several times a day in your mind you *will* gradually begin to tolerate it.

The trouble is that the phobic person does not want to add to her continuing distress by forcing herself to experience further suffering. 'Who will make me better?' they plead, not accepting that there is much they can do themselves.

Of course it should be possible for severely phobic patients to receive specialist treatment at hospital, but this is rarely available except in very few areas; further, when hospitals *can* offer treatment there may often be a wait of up to two years. This is why it is so important to understand the basics of self help.

# ALL CREATURES GREAT AND SMALL

It is easy to understand how a person might develop a phobia about a certain animal when an episode in their childhood may have upset them to such an extent that they are left with a permanent fear. Strangely enough, these phobias are rarely 'passed on' by an adult. The fact that a mother has a cat phobia might result in her children being wary of the animals or disliking them but it is unlikely they themselves will become phobic.

Being bitten by a snarling dog or damaged by the claws of a cat can leave a permanent imprint on the mind of a child. Because of the fear she will avoid the animal and the fear will remain into adulthood. If she finds herself near to a dog or cat her body language and her scent signal *fear*, which the creature quickly senses and reacts to, sometimes with aggression, more often with curiosity.

The following is a list of animals to which many people are phobic. In each case, I have noted the possible reasons for the phobia (although obviously, the initiating fears are different for everyone) along with some measures that you can adopt to help you control it. If your phobia forces you to alter your lifestyle in any way, now is the time to attack it.

## Cats

How often does someone who is afraid of cats insist that a cat will always make a beeline for them, singling them out in a crowded room to weave around their legs and even try to jump on to their laps? And other people may experience a genuine physical reaction, as you can see from the case below.

> I don't have to see a cat to know that one is in the room. Apart from a deadly fear of the creatures my body reacts physically and I feel nauseated, a rash erupts on the back of my hands and my breathing is affected. Above all, when I come face to face with a cat it is the eyes that terrify me. They have an unblinking stare that bores into you as if the animal knows what you are thinking ...

Cats *do* often make a beeline for people who feel fear or distaste. Animals like to please and when they sense antipathy or dislike, they try to right that with affection. This, in the eyes of the sufferer, can be perceived as an assault, or a purposeful attempt by the animal to aggravate. In the case above, it is possible that the sufferer's 'physical reaction' is a genuine allergy to the animal. When he breaks out in physical symptoms, like a rash, he may blame this on the intensity of his fear rather than on a chemical reaction. By treating this medically – or better yet, homoeopathically – one aspect of his reaction to cats will be removed, making it easier to tackle the psychological symptoms.

When you determine to take the first step in tackling your phobia, try some of the following:

● First of all try to get your feelings of anxiety under control with the breathing and relaxation techniques we discussed earlier (see pages 113–118). Remember that 'over-breathing' upsets the chemical balance in your system, and in itself this will cause increasing anxiety which can escalate into a panic attack.

● Then – here comes the crunch – you *must* try to develop a more positive attitude towards your phobic object.

● Write it down. Write six statements about cats, then take a look at your list. It will probably run something like this:

> A cat is a sly, untrustworthy creature;
> it has evil connections with the underworld;
> you never know which way it is going to jump;
> it stares at you with unblinking eyes;
> I fear it may bite or scratch me;
> it has disgusting toilet and cleaning habits.

● Now *force* yourself to write down six *nice* things about them. For instance:

> Kittens are pretty playful creatures and grow into affectionate, playful pets;
> a cat's fur is soft and strokable;
> the cat has been admired in myth and legend;
> cats are among the cleanest and most fastidious of creatures;
> a cat would be frightened of me and would run away if I shouted at it;
> cats can be the warmest and gentlest of pets.

The idea is that you develop a positive attitude towards the cat. Throw away your negative list and concentrate on the second one – and try to think of even more good things to say about cats. Look at pictures of pretty kittens, watch the TV commercials of gentle, affectionate cats waiting for their meal. You will *not* like doing this but it is a step you have to take. The next steps will be even more difficult:

• Touch and even cuddle a toy cat, carrying it around with you until you become used to it. Progressing towards tolerating a real cat will, of course, be more difficult. For one thing, it moves.

The next step to take is to experiment with approaching the cats. Test your theory:

• Approach a cat in the street and shoo it away. Once you've accepted that you are in control, the cat will certainly seem less fearsome.

• When you are able to try out another experiment, *speak* to the cat in the street. Nine times out of ten it will 'talk' back to you and make a friendly approach. You can then walk away or stroke its head and find out how responsive it is.

• All the time, appreciate that you are in control, and the more you practise getting used to the animal the easier it will get.

I have concentrated on the cat to illustrate the basic approach to the phobic problem. The same techniques can apply to any other animal.

## Dogs

Dog phobias are becoming more and more common since the bad publicity they have received recently and it is sad but true that there are many more aggressive dogs about than there used to be. On the whole, though, the problem is more often likely to be a perfectly reasonable fear of being attacked and bitten than an irrational terror.

However, to someone who suffers from 'cynophobia', fear of dogs, it does not matter whether a dog is a ravenous rottweiler or a cuddly cocker spaniel, the terror is the same. If you have a dog phobia you should go about tackling it in the same way as described for a cat phobia:

• Direct your mind to thinking positively about the dog

- Control your anxiety with breath control exercises
- If you can progress to touching and handling a puppy, it would be a step forward, but I would not suggest touching an adult dog for some time and then only if the owner has it on a leash – not because it might be dangerous but because many dogs are over-friendly and boisterous and this could be unsettling
- Even when you are more confident, don't approach a dog in the street, as you might a cat, and don't stare into a dog's eyes as it will interpret this as an aggressive challenge.

Occasionally, a dog phobia can be triggered off by loud barking. Many anxiety-prone, over-sensitive people over-react to a sudden loud noise. The subject might well interpret this as a reaction to the dog itself and not just the sound of its barking.

There is a story of one woman's attempt to cure herself of her dog phobia. She summoned up the courage to buy a puppy, left it in her house while she went out shopping – and then was too afraid to go back into the house. One hopes that after such a promising start she was later able to proceed with her determination to overcome the phobia.

## Birds

Consider how disabling a fear of birds can be. After all, they are everywhere – even the big cities are swarming with them. In mainline stations there are notices telling people not to feed or encourage the birds. In London squares, tourists buy bags of birdseed with which to feed the pigeons who obligingly alight on hands and heads and pose for photographs. Unfortunately, they get so used to doing this that they fly hopefully in the direction of anyone in the vicinity.

Laura has had to give up her job in the centre of London and now rarely goes out of the house except to shop or socialize after dark:

> I cannot go into my garden without my radio, which I play as loud as I can. I have three Persian cats which, unlike other cats, are clumsy and slothful and unable to move fast enough to catch any-

thing bigger than a butterfly. They are, however, very useful because they patrol the garden and keep the birds away. I could not cope with an ordinary cat which might bring dead birds into the house.

Again, many of the birds' characteristics are the reason for the fear. Beady eyes, scaly claws, the darting beaks and fluttering wings – oh, and feathers. There are many feather phobics and sometimes this is linked with an actual fear of birds, though in other cases it is the feathers that cause horror. 'They get up your nose and suffocate you', 'They fly in all directions', and 'They seem somehow unreal' are some of the complaints of a feather phobic. Feathers are in pillows and cushions, and on hats. They can drift into sight unexpectedly. 'Butchers' shops at Christmas are horrific for me. I can eat turkey if I haven't seen it in its natural state, but I'm having roast beef for my Christmas dinner.'

So, what to do about it?

● If the problem is birds, but includes a fear of feathers, tackle the feather fear first. Though you are repelled by the thought of touching one, though the sensation on your skin is distressing, you must acclimatize yourself gradually.

Annette, a thirty-five-year-old mother, has a horror of feathers which she feels is at the root of her dislike of birds. She found it very difficult at first to touch a real feather but has persisted, carrying around a tiny fluffy feather initially and then handling larger ones.

● Birdsong? Try listening to records or cassettes. John, aged twelve, is getting used to the cries of seagulls – a sound whose 'dreadful melancholy' made him cry uncontrollably.

## Other Flying Creatures

Bats, butterflies and moths are particularly common phobic objects. The fear is often of sudden contact – bats getting entangled in hair, butterflies or moths alighting on one's hand and fluttering. Again, the sudden movements cause acute anxiety.

Approach your fear of flying creatures in much the same way as outlined for cats. Try watching wildlife programmes centred on the species that frightens you. Obviously these kinds of animals are untameable and therefore unpredictable, so their sporadic fluttering or flying might always be slightly disconcerting; but if you remember that they are harmless, and perhaps teach yourself to appreciate their unique qualities, you should soon be able to tolerate them.

## Mice and Other Small Creatures

The trouble with these creatures is that they 'scuttle'. I have mentioned that very over-sensitized people over-react to loud noises, while others may similarly react to sudden movement, which makes them jump and again can trigger off a panic attack.

It is important to concentrate on breathing and relaxation before pushing yourself any further. Like flying creatures mice are quite unpredictable, even when tamed, so acclimatizing and conditioning yourself not to receive a fright with every movement is the key to successfully overcoming a rodent phobia.

You might also try:

- Visiting your local pet shop, and tentatively watching baby mice or hamsters in their cages. They are much less mobile under those circumstances.
- Watching programmes, or reading up on your phobic object. Certainly getting to know its habits and 'personality' will make it easier to understand, and therefore less frightening.
- Petting a guinea pig, or another larger, less sporadic member of the rodent family. When you get used to their looks, feel and habits, the smaller members of the family will not be quite so intimidating.
- The same tips as you would for a cat phobia, and take it slowly.

Remember that you don't actually ever have to *like* these animals – you just want to conquer your fear of them. Avoiding something because you don't like it is certainly different and less disruptive than avoiding something because it terrorizes you, and takes over your life.

An animal phobia can be beaten. Don't despair.

## Spiders

After a recent documentary programme on television, I received nearly eight hundred letters. While the majority were from agoraphobia sufferers, among them many were from people who are afraid of dozens of different animals, illnesses and objects. Sixty-seven were from people afraid of spiders.

Spider phobias are common, and there are a number of steps you can take to overcome one:

- Exposure therapy at a hospital. You would proceed very slowly, the therapist taking you through minute details one at a time. This kind of therapy will take many sessions, so if you are trying to do it yourself, *don't* push yourself too quickly.
- Writing your list. Your positive list of *nice* things you can think of about spiders may be difficult to compile, but persevere. Tell yourself that a spider's web is a beautiful and intricate piece of engineering, that a spider is a beautifully designed living machine and has as much right to its share of the planet as you have. There are no dangerous spiders in this country, and any spider is much more frightened of you than you should be of it.

You must change your attitude towards spiders:

- Think kindly of them
- Look at pictures in books
- Go into the garden early in the morning and wonder at the beauty of a newly spun web with the dew on it.

The disruptive part of any phobia is not the fear of something when you encounter it but the dragging, nerve-racking hours you spend in anticipation of the moment you do have to face it. Banish that irrational fear from your mind and you'll be amazed how worry-free your life can be. Again, you don't ever have to like or be comfortable around spiders. What you do have to do is learn to let them play no part in your day-to-day life.

# Snakes

It does not matter that you are unlikely to come across a snake during the course of the day; to the phobic person the very thought of a snake induces feelings not just of revulsion and dislike but panic, nausea and overwhelming horror. Imagine what effect the following statement must have had on those who spend their lives avoiding anything where a snake just might be mentioned.

Fred, a six-foot python who escaped from a South London pet shop four days ago, has been found in the kitchen of a house less than a hundred metres from his home. Little Jason Paul who found the snake was very upset when his mother told him he could not keep it as a pet. 'But he loves me,' wailed Jason as Fred coiled lovingly around his neck.

*South East London Mercury*

Many of those with a snake phobia have never seen a snake, and it is believed that the human race has an innate fear of snakes. Many animals also have this fear – monkeys brought up in captivity without ever seeing a snake still act fearfully when shown one. This example shows how such a dormant fear can be brought to life:

I'm not sure when my phobia started but I have a picture in my mind – which I must have seen in a book when I was a child – of a snake dislocating its lower jaw in order to swallow a small animal, which was disappearing down its throat. I have never seen anything so evil in my life, though I try to tell myself it is just another of God's creatures behaving normally. But those vicious fangs and those baleful glittering eyes! The picture remains in my mind today. I avoid looking at books which might contain pictures of snakes. I never watch wildlife programmes on television and I would certainly never go near the reptile house at the zoo.

If you are prepared to try to overcome a snake phobia – that is, your horror of books, pictures, any mention of the creature – there is one important point to remember. If you live in

134

Britain, it is ninety-eight per cent certain that you will *never* see a snake. That being so, you do not have to touch one or even face one when you are tackling your fear. Not in real life, that is. The fear you have to overcome is in your own imagination. That is what you have to get under control.

Try the same tips as for 'Flying Creatures', page 132. Exposure therapy – which may never involve actually seeing a live snake – is the key. Take it slowly and gently acclimatize yourself through books and pictures. If you have to travel to a country in which the chances of seeing a live snake are more likely, try some of the therapies listed in Chapter 5. Hypnotherapy can be particularly helpful when an overwhelming fear threatens to take over your thoughts. Because, as mentioned, humans and other animals may have an intrinsic fear of snakes, professional help may be your best option.

Can movies, television plays and video films be a source of phobia-provoking reactions? Might people not develop a life-long fear after watching a film about giant spiders, horrific insects, snakes, reptiles and other nasties? Probably not, as it is unlikely that any anxious, highly sensitized person would dream of watching such a film.

On the other hand, thousands of people were disturbed by the film *Jaws* because of the sheer unexpectedness of the horror scenes. The situations in the film started as normal and everyday happenings which escalated into an explosive shock. The background music, monotonous and synchronized with the throb of a heart beat was deliberately anxiety provoking. Coupled with the shock of a sudden horror scene, the screams of the audience were enough to trigger off panic attacks, fainting and a wholesale stampede out of the cinema. It is not surprising that many who saw the film developed an aversion to sea bathing.

More seriously, real cases of shark phobias developing were reported from phobia organizations in the USA and Britain. And these phobias were disrupting lives. Obviously not everyone who watched the film developed a phobia, but certainly a fear of sharks was introduced to each viewer's mind. If you are easily frightened by programmes or books of this nature, or if you are just highly sensitive or imaginative, just avoid them. The titillating thrill of being frightened within the safe confines of the cinema soon loses its attraction when upsetting images and nightmares start entering your consciousness.

## SHOES AND SHIPS AND SEALING WAX

Whatever the object, situation, illness, animal or natural phenomenon, somebody somewhere has a phobia of it. Some are so odd that the sufferers go through life never admitting to them and never imagining that they could receive treatment, let alone tackle the problem themselves.

I could fill the rest of the book listing all the phobias from which people suffer, but here are just a few I have come across in the Open Door and PAX:

| | |
|---|---|
| leaves | disfigurement |
| flowers | books |
| the number thirteen | eyes |
| buses | musical instruments |
| dolls | ghosts |
| garden gnomes | snow |
| cotton wool | knives |
| midgets | needles |

It is difficult for a non-phobic person to appreciate how devastating these fears can be. And it's difficult to understand that the phobic person is probably completely normal and not mentally deranged. Probably? Of course, there are many mental patients who suffer from phobias as well as their particular illness but just because someone is phobic does not mean that *they* are suffering from a mental illness.

Remember the theory behind the basis of a phobia: 'The sufferer externalizes her or his feelings of anxiety by projecting them on to a specific object or situation which itself becomes the problem.'

Whether it is an animal or an object that is the cause of the

136

phobia, it must be overcome by gradual exposure. For example, consider this doll phobia.

Janice has had a fear of dolls from infancy. This may not sound too upsetting but consider the ramifications if you are married and want a child. This was Janice's original letter:

> My aunt felt she could 'cure' my phobia by buying a cheap doll and pulling off its head, arms and legs in front of me, just to prove it was an inanimate object. That made me ten times worse. I have to cross the road when there is a toy shop on one side, and though I choose very carefully which television programmes to watch I have to leave the room when there are commercials involving toys, especially at Christmas.
>
> I have tried to overcome this phobia and my husband tries to understand but he now thinks we should start a family and I cannot face the idea. Supposing I had a little girl? She would want to play with dolls and a boy would want soldiers and other character dolls. I could not tolerate them in the house, but I'm afraid my husband will get fed up and I don't know what to do.

Janice decided to try hypnotherapy which helped her to relax and also to cope with a number of anxieties which came to the surface. However, the doll phobia remained, and Janice set about making a determined attempt to overcome it. She cut out pictures of children from magazines and Christmas cards, keeping them in a cardboard box and handling them every day. She then progressed to pictures of dolls, which she added to the collection.

'I don't like them at all,' she wrote to the PAX newsletter, 'but I know that avoiding them means I will never get used to them. My next step is to try a rag doll which is less threatening than one that looks too human.'

On a personal note, from childhood I had a horror of skeletons, skulls and bones. Churchyards and cemeteries aroused feelings of terror and a holiday at a country house hotel when I was ten years old was ruined as the owner, who had been a big-game hunter, had the skulls of his trophies mounted all around the dining room with green light bulbs inside them. The fear increased until I could not read an adventure book or go to a movie where there might be a skeleton. I don't mean horror films, even something as apparently non-threatening as *Treasure Island* could be guaranteed to have me fleeing from the cinema when the buried treasure was discovered, guarded by a grinning skeleton.

Even at school I was not safe as there was a skull in the corner of the art studio. I would find a seat as far from that corner as possible. Outings to museums filled me with dread as there was bound to be a plethora of bones lurking in the natural history section. A boyfriend once tried to persuade me to go into a little country museum and carried me inside kicking and yelling. I never spoke to him again.

I did eventually shed that particular phobia. It took a long time – several years – but I had to learn that avoidance made things worse and that I needed to learn to face up to looking at and touching bones. I even forced myself to listen to a silly song that for years had made me feel ill: '*The leg bone connected to the ankle bone . . . dem bones, dem bones goin' to walk around.*' I still have a little shudder when I see a skeleton.

Some elderly people have phobias that have persisted through life, and to which they have never admitted. Most would never have imagined that they could receive treatment, never mind having an idea of how to tackle the problems themselves. Even colours, because of some early association, can produce a life-long fear.

I came across one old lady with a phobia of the colour purple and of purple flowers, in particular. She thought it had something to do with funerals and mourning, and it was discovered that it stemmed from when she was very young, when her formidable grandmother – who was always in mourning for some relative – always wore long purple and black dresses.

Today it is simply not necessary for a phobia to last a lifetime. The first step – inclination – to remove a phobia from your life is already there. No one *wants* to suffer from a phobia, no matter how lightly it may affect your day-to-day life. And it's important to remember that any kind of phobia can be overcome, even those that are intangible, as we'll see in the next chapter.

# 10

# INTANGIBLE FEARS AND PHOBIAS

Most of us suffer to some degree from intangible fears, whether they be fears of heights or darkness, or even space. Intangible fears are, therefore, more socially acceptable simply because they are more understood, and shared. The problem arises when a fear develops into a phobia.

Like tangible phobias, however, intangible phobias *can* be conquered, and often with a series of self-help measures. Once you know what your fears are, you begin to cure them.

The following constitute some of the most common fears and phobias, and wherever possible, I've included some very simple self-help steps to overcome them.

## Fear of Flying

Fear of flying can affect *anyone*, even the strongest and the bravest. It is important to point out that among the reported thirty million people in Britain and the USA who suffer from air-travel anxiety, a fairly small proportion can be said to have a flying *phobia*. They may certainly be very very frightened, but the fears they experience are usually pretty understandable and, when faced up to, can be dealt with.

Understanding the mechanics of flying is a step to allaying the normal anxieties in the minds of most people. Air Travel Anxiety Seminars have lectures on the construction and operation of the aircraft – answering the question at the back of many people's minds: '*How* does it fly?' Acclimatizing prospective passengers to the mysteries of flying, particularly those who have never flown before, is the aim of several airlines who run 'no-go' flights. A report in one of the PAX newsletter encouraged other members to try a 'flight to nowhere'.

This is exactly like going on a real flight except that the plane doesn't leave the ground. You book your ticket and, arriving at the airport, you check in and wait for your flight to be called. In the departure lounge the captain and crew talk about their training and exactly what they do during a typical flight. They explain about the aircraft and answer questions.

In many cases agoraphobia and claustrophobia are the main problem, not just the experience of flying. There is a concern about what might happen to themselves – panic or a lack of control. 'What if I can't bear the feeling of being trapped?' the sufferer might think. 'What if I have a full scale panic attack? I might scream or faint or make an exhibition of myself.' There is little point in trying to overcome a flying fear until the basic agoraphobia or claustrophobia have been brought under control. Ex-sufferers *do* fly.

Dr Yaffé, in his book *Taking the Fear Out of Flying* suggests that people practise certain exercises to prepare themselves for flying. The situations simulate as closely as possible sensations similar to those experienced when actually flying and point out where coping strategies can be applied. For instance, travelling on a crowded Underground train or high-speed lift. For those with a fear of heights, they are told to get acclimatized by looking from the top of high buildings, or a bridge where they can look over the edge.

You will appreciate that to overcome all the varied fears that can make up a flying phobia you will have to do an awful lot of groundwork.

Airlines do try to ensure that the atmosphere in a plane is as soothing as possible. There are usually in-flight films and piped music as well as food and drinks. Cabin staff are trained to help nervous passengers and to notice if anyone becomes distressed or panicky. Strangely enough, when a phobic person feels able to make a flight they don't feel so anxious once the plane has actually taken off. The dreadful time of anticipation is past, and that is the worst part for a phobic sufferer.

# Heights

When fear of heights is mentioned you probably visualize standing on the top of a high building or at the edge of a cliff and
experiencing a sensation of being drawn over. Imagination plays
a large part in this, of course. If you shut your eyes and walk
along an imaginary line on the floor you will find it simple. But
visualize a tightrope fifty feet above the ground and it will be
virtually impossible to walk along that line. When we are in a
situation where we are high up we imagine – no, we *see* –
ourselves drawn towards the edge; we see ourselves plummet-
ting downwards and the inevitable consequences.

A fear of falling is a fear of loss of support, says Isaac Marks.
More precisely, it is fear of loss of *visual* support. But I know
people who cannot be in a room on an upper floor of a building
unless the curtains are closed. A window offers no protection
to them.

'I could climb the highest tree when I was young, stand on
the top of a tall building or even climb a cliff and feel not the
least qualm,' is a common statement of sufferers. It does appear
that many a fear of heights doesn't develop until middle age.
In these cases it could have something to do with the fact that
inner-ear disorders occur in a huge number of people in later
life, causing dizziness and feelings of disorientation. Gradually,
the phobia can develop. Fear of heights can overwhelm the
sufferer as much as any other phobia. If allowed, it can take
over the waking – and sleeping – hours of the individual. One
sufferer noted:

> I have this recurring dream of climbing to the top of a high rock
> or an edifice such as a huge chimney. I am perfectly all right going
> up but on reaching the top find it impossible to climb down again
> and there is no way I can be rescued. I wake in a cold sweat and
> suffering from acute vertigo.

A somewhat different fear of heights is that of looking *up*
rather than looking down. Again, this may well have a physical
foundation. If your balancing mechanism is out of kilter you
will feel dizzy if you tilt your head and look upwards. Your

eyes may then play tricks and this is when high buildings appear to lean towards you, creating a feeling of unsteadiness and a need to hang on to the nearest support.

I recently had a letter from a young woman who had projected her fears on to two specific buildings: the Empire State Building and the Eiffel Tower. She had never seen them and probably never would but every waking moment these buildings were on her mind. Of course they appeared to grow bigger and bigger the more she thought about them until she imagined them as 'touching the sky'. Needless to say, she also dreamed about them and would awake feeling sick and dizzy with fright. It was, she said, a situation which no one could understand; it seemed so ridiculous to be afraid of two buildings she had never seen.

## Space

Space phobia is more common than one might suppose. I don't mean science fiction, astronauts and spaceships, although I wouldn't be surprised if the thought of these didn't strike horror into a few people's hearts. The concept of infinity is overwhelming and space phobia sufferers often can not bear to look up into the sky or look at the stars at night.

A woman went to a friend's house one night when the conversation turned to space travel, astronauts orbiting the planet and how the Earth itself was spinning in space. On her way home the woman felt that she could see the sky flying past and that she was about to fall off the Earth. Her friends helped her home where she collapsed in great distress with a panic attack. She did not leave her house for two years.

There are other cases of space phobia that I have come across. None of the sufferers was able to get professional help – apart from tranquillizers – and as these were normal, well-balanced people they were loath to talk about their fears. Those with height phobias were also invariably normal in other ways – not especially over-sensitive, no anxiety problems in early life – so it is not surprising that they felt resentful at being labelled 'neurotic' by their medical advisors. Dizzy feelings are interpreted by doctors as an antecedent to anxiety. Everyone I have known insists that dizziness *precedes* anxiety and panic attacks.

At the Dizziness and Balance Center in Illinois, Dr Jeffrey Kramer quoted statistics from the National Institute for Mental Health. In his view, dizziness is the second most common complaint people bring to doctors. Forty-two per cent of adults report episodes of dizziness or vertigo to their physician at some time in their lives. Eighty-five per cent of dizziness is caused by disorders of the vestibular system in the inner ear. When someone feels dizzy he feels he is out of control and this can cause anxiety and panic.

Once the sufferer understands *why* she feels afraid she can learn to control the fear of the fear. Breathing exercises to counteract hyperventilation, and relaxation will help to cope with the dizzy spells.

Other phobias which have a similar background are 'elemental phobias': sunshine, clouds and large expanses of water may cause the phobic person to feel disoriented. Many of these phobias would never come to light were it not for the phobia organizations and the occasional TV programme or magazine article which persuades people to talk about unusual fears.

It is rare for these sufferers to seek help, as they are afraid of being labelled 'odd', and worried, if they confide in their GPs, that they may be persuaded to take tranquillizers or labelled difficult and uncooperative if they refuse.

To admit to having a fear of clouds does not usually engender a very sympathetic response. One sufferer explains the feeling:

My particular phobia is open sky and clouds. I am happiest on a grey day, even if it is raining, as I can go out quite happily sheltering under an umbrella. I sometimes think I must have been a tortoise or a snail in a past life!

Somehow a canopy of blue sky stretching endlessly over the horizon makes me feel unsafe and dizzy. I don't mind fluffy white clouds, if they are not moving much, but when they are scuttling across the sky I can't bear to look up. My real horror is the huge black thunderheads looming overhead. This may sound trivial but even writing about them makes me feel ill.

Sunshine and blue skies cause distress for many who can not tolerate brightness and space, and who prefer to go out shopping when supermarkets are open late in the evening.

But what about the dark?

# Darkness

I feel that a grown man should not have to make such an admission but I have a horror of nighttime. I find that the dark has an oppressive quality – it seems to bear down heavily on me and I feel suffocated. Living in a large town I am all right going out at night because of the lights, but there is no way I could ever live in the country. There are several security lights in my garden so I am surrounded by a ring of light, but my protection is not so much against intruders but against the black night.

Donald had five years of psychoanalysis but made no progress with his darkness fears. He did benefit from the insight he gained into his inner feelings. 'The best advice I received,' he wrote, 'was to stop worrying about the problem and tell myself that I didn't have to ever face total darkness. This acceptance has lifted most of my feelings of anxiety.'

Other darkness phobics can try overcoming the problem by slowly exposing themselves to darker circumstances.

# Wind and Weather

The district organizer of the Thanet Phobic Group told the PAX newsletter, 'Since the hurricane in 1987 many people developed a fear of high winds . . . 1990 brought us still more, and near-hurricane-force winds, so that more people have developed quite serious phobias. When a gale is forecast they are reduced to nervous wrecks waiting for the prophesized wind to arrive. One sufferer told me, "In a way the worst part is after the forecast, waiting for the storm to arrive." '

Never have so many people watched and listened to the weather forecasts. As soon as high winds are promised, mattresses are moved downstairs and people sleep in whichever room is not facing the way the wind is blowing. They wear earplugs, headphones and listen to music – anything that will blot out the sound of the howling winds, crashing tiles and breaking glass.

After the great hurricane of 1987 the streets of Britain resembled her war-torn years, with debris everywhere. This happened in other countries, too, of course, but Britain had never experienced such extreme weather conditions and confidence in weather predictability was fast dissipating. People now talk of 'having a quiet night last night', just as they did in wartime. One young man sleeps under a table where he feels safe. Even more distressing, some people are afraid to go to work when the wind is blowing.

It has been suggested that relaxation techniques will help to control the anxiety. I think what frightens people the most is the helplessness they feel at not being able to 'turn off' the thing that is frightening them.

Another contact wrote:

> I would rather have gone through a cold dark winter with low temperatures and heavy snow than this unseasonal warm weather we have been experiencing and the dreadful gales that regularly blow up. I find my whole nervous system is over-reacting to the high winds and I feel over-strung, like a twisted rubber band. I've always had trouble with thunder but this is almost worse. It's not that I'm worried about storm damage or crashing trees; this fear seems to be much more elemental.

For hundreds of years winds have been blamed for upsetting man's equilibrium. Spenser described the north wind as 'bitter, black and blustering', and Shakespeare called it 'wrathful and tyrannous', holding it responsible for 'gout, the falling evil, itch and the ague'. Hundreds of years earlier, Hippocrates was convinced that people exposed to west winds became pale and sickly, with digestive organs that were 'frequently deranged from the phlegm that runs down into them from the head'.

It is likely that there have been wind problems around for a long time and that there is nothing new about them. However, in twenty-five years and with nearly forty thousand contacts since I started the Open Door, I have not come across so many people suffering from this problem. It has not been publicized for the simple reason that sufferers endure the fear and keep silent about it.

With the help of self-help groups throughout the country I managed to find fifty wind phobia sufferers. Thirty-four were men, of no specific age group, and though both male and female sufferers had a history of phobia problems, only a few of them had a serious fear of wind before the gales of recent years. Now they feel their lives have indeed been affected and some fear they could become housebound if the anticipatory anxiety they experience increases.

It has long been known that certain winds peculiar to particular areas of the world can cause strange mental and physical sensations, and with changing atmospheric conditions we too are now feeling the effects of strange winds. These so-called 'witches' winds' around the world have been shown to increase the number of road accidents, violent crimes, suicides and murders and so have led to an interest about the electricity in the air.

In *Heaven's Breath, A Natural History of the Wind*, Lyall Watson wrote:

> There is no doubt that days with a lot of wind were once dangerous ones, destroying shelters, dispersing warning scents and masking the sound of an approaching predator. And it may be that even in our modern climate we are still excited and disturbed by the old signals. The physiology seems to involve the classic alarm reaction of increased production of adrenalin. Metabolism speeds up, blood vessels of the heart and muscles dilate, skin vessels contract, the pupils widen and the hair shows a disturbing tendency to stand on end, producing prickles of apprehension. This is a fine and useful response to an emergency, a good prelude to instant action; but when it is provoked by an alarm that goes on ringing, by a wind that blows for hours or even days on end, it puts a lot of strain on the system.

Certainly, the reaction to wind which our bodies undergo without our mental instructions can be very frightening. And we begin to fear that out-of-control feeling. Fear of the fear again.

It is not just the wind that people are afraid of, but the physical sensations that occur when the wind is blowing. When this is understood, much of the anxiety fades.

Again, anxiety control is important. It is impossible to organize winds in small amounts so one can learn to gradually desensitize oneself; however, from later reports from some of the fifty sufferers already mentioned, this is a problem that wears itself out in time.

# Thunderstorms

People have always been nervous of thunderstorms. Of course there is reason to be fearful – they can cause damage, even death, in a few cases though the odds are that you would be more likely to meet your end in a road accident. But these are not the reasons why phobic anxiety develops about thunder. Those who suffer from general anxiety states and have an over-sensitized nervous system are going to be increasingly sensitive when there are changes in the atmosphere. Anxiety rises and they ask themselves, 'Why am I feeling so frightened? I must be afraid of *something*. The wind is building up, the weather forecast predicts thunderstorms; I am feeling worse and worse so it must be the thunder that makes me feel this way.'

Apart from the physiological reaction, the thunder-phobic person has probably had these fears since childhood, likely derived from observing the behaviour of adults who were also afraid of storms.

One thunder phobic notes:

I used to stay with two aunts who became hysterical when there was a thunderstorm. They would hide in a cupboard and, of course, take me in with them and we would stay there sometimes for hours expecting at every moment that our last hour had come. Unfortunately, the fears I acquired in childhood have worsened through the years. I avoid looking at weather forecasts on the television but if I do get an inkling that thunder is on the way my apprehension gets quite out of control. All I want is for the blessed storm to arrive and get it over so that I can feel normal again.

Some phobia experts advise against studying the weather

forecasts so that anticipatory anxiety is less likely to build up, but someone who is severely affected has no need to check the forecasts. His or her body is already sending out warning signals.

Hyper-sensitive people can become overwhelmed by the disturbing stimuli of light and sound. Where there is a concentration of noise and bright light the stimulus can get too much and the over-sensitized nervous system will 'blow a fuse'; in other words, trigger off a panic attack. The sufferer knows how she is going to feel during the storm and waiting for it to arrive is almost worse than the actual event.

Here we have to understand the defective perception of time that the sufferers of severe anticipatory anxiety experience. During a thunderstorm the period between the lightning flash and the crash of thunder can seem endless. The subject asks herself, 'When is it coming? Will I be able to bear it? Will the noise be too great for my ears or my nervous system to tolerate?' The agonizing stress builds up and up and when she finds that she has survived the crash she will start to anticipate the next cycle.

It is the anticipation, the waiting, that causes the greatest distress. If you are a sufferer check this out next time. When do you feel worse? When the lightning flashes? When the thunder rolls? Or during the time when you are awaiting the arrival of the storm? The wait for the first flash of lightning can seem intolerably long and the intervals in between the flash and the thunderclap leave time for anxiety to escalate again and again.

Those of you with 'elemental phobias' – thunder, lightning or wind, etc. – should recognize that some of your apprehension may well be caused by an over-sensitive nervous system reacting to changes in the atmosphere. Realizing this, you can then try to control the anxiety with correct breathing and relaxation instead of letting it take hold of you and escalate into a panic attack when you have seen storm warnings on television.

*Coping techniques:* Weather forecast sends you into a spin? Try these tips:

- Sit in an easy chair or lie on your bed. Loosen your clothes and place your finger tips together on your diaphragm. Breathe correctly (from the bottom of your lungs); done properly, your fingers should part.
- Creative visualization: try to see your house surrounded by a protective light, telling yourself that you are quite safe, that the sound and light cannot harm you. Remember to think positively. It works.

Creative visualisation and some of the alternative complementary therapies might help you to tackle an intangible phobia. Understanding how the phobia developed is important so that the 'fear of the fear' can be tackled. PAX has produced a cassette called 'Overcoming Thunder and Weather Phobias', which you may also find useful.

# 11

# AFRAID TO BE ILL?

How well do you understand your body and all its functions? Most of us are pretty ignorant and often we prefer not to know too much until something goes wrong and we fearfully present ourselves at the doctor's surgery.

We are well instructed by the media about what we should and should not do to keep healthy, and we are left in little doubt about some of the awful things that can go wrong if we smoke, eat the wrong things, get too fat or too thin, or exercise too little or too much. We are told to feel our breasts for lumps, undergo smear tests and X-rays and present ourself for regular health checks, blood pressure, and, perhaps, cholesterol and blood sugar level tests. We read alarming accounts in every magazine of new and unnerving medical procedures, and personal stories describing how someone has suffered and survived every physical and mental disorder under the sun – with all the detailed descriptions of symptoms. What a minefield for the anxious person and potential phobia sufferer!

You too have probably examined every little mole on your body after a fortnight in the sun, or wondered whether that mouth ulcer was cancerous, what *is* causing that darting pain, that niggling ache, those dizzy spells or that persistent cough?

Of course it is necessary to be careful about these things and get them checked out, but nine times out of ten we are worrying about nothing at all and the problem can often be dealt with with a few words of reassurance.

People with illness phobias need to be distinguished from hypochondriacs, who have many imagined symptoms and illnesses. Phobics focus on one particular illness and any symptoms experienced point in only one direction – to the disease they so dread. The differences between hypochondria and phobia are illustrated below:

## Phobias

- Dread and anticipation of contracting a specific illness
- Apart from the symptoms of acute, continuing anxiety the subject knows they are not ill
- The phobic person does not gain from the phobia, unlike the hypochondriac
- Most will go out of their way to hide their fears and only when desperate will submit to medical tests which still will not convince them that the dreaded disease is not apparent.

## Hypochondria

- Constant worry about ill-health generally
- Anticipation does not play an important part but symptoms of any illness will cause the person to rush to the doctor for reassurance. They usually accept this until symptoms of another illness appear
- They sometimes convince themselves that they *are* ill and seek sympathy and attention from others
- They may even appear to enjoy the situation.

Fear of the unknown and fear of the fear. I have shown how these are the causes of many phobic states. A generally anxious person with an over-active imagination is most likely to develop an illness phobia if she has had some contact with a particular disease. Perhaps a member of her family had cancer, perhaps an acquaintance has died after a heart attack. As her convictions that she is experiencing similar symptoms strengthen, the signals of stress become more evident – with racing pulse, over-breathing and aches and pains due to muscle tension.

She becomes so terrified at the thought of the illness that she will avoid any mention of it, never watching television programmes that feature hospitals. In very severe cases, even newspapers are barred in case the word, the name of the illness is printed. Oh yes, many phobic people can not bear to see their phobia mentioned. (In the seventies, one member of the Open Door insisted that I blocked out the word *dentist* in her newsletters.)

Those who have never suffered from a phobia cannot imagine how this can dominate the life of a sufferer *every waking hour*.

It would be pointless to try and discuss every illness phobia, as the list would take up pages and pages. These phobias are among the most difficult to treat and it is important that sufferers *do* try to get professional help as there are sometimes underlying psychological problems that need to be uncovered and dealt with by experts.

Self help in this area is very much a first-aid operation, really aimed at encouraging the sufferer to face up to the problem and take the next step in seeking professional advice.

First of all, we will look at just some of the most common phobias, then some of the things you can do to help yourself.

## Cancer Phobia

This is the most common illness phobia. It is, of course, important that we all know how to ensure that we have a healthy lifestyle and do not put ourselves in a dangerous position where we might be vulnerable to cancerous diseases. In recent years, the dangers of cigarette smoking and too much sunshine have received a great deal of exposure in the media, but one has to balance the usefulness of such publicity in demonstrating that something positive can be done to avoid certain types of cancer with the distress and fear it can induce among thousands of anxiety-prone people.

'One in twelve women will contract breast cancer,' shout posters and magazine articles. What they do not make clear is that most cancers develop after middle-age; a woman of thirty looking at her friends of the same age and thinking *one of us will get breast cancer* is misinformed. If you were to take twelve women whose ages ranged from thirty to eighty it would be reasonable to assume that one of them would be in danger of having breast cancer at some time.

The healer Matthew Manning blames a cancer phobia epidemic on the media, feeling that this is partially due to the regular flow of publicity about the large numbers of people who die from cancer.

> Too often we neglect the fact that thousands of people each year *do* survive cancer because of medical intervention, complementary therapies and the sheer determination of the individual patient. However this is not often given publicity. We are not helped either by the fact that certainly until fairly recently much of the advertising for funds, not only for cancer research but for many other serious and potentially life-threatening illnesses, has relied heavily on presenting a dark and gloomy picture. The point that some of my patients make is that if you only present the blackest statistics you are likely to foster a negative response to the disease. If for example a woman discovers a lump in her breast and is told by a consultant that she has cancer, having seen advertising suggesting that "cancer is a killer disease" she is immediately at an emotional disadvantage.

Sir Macfarlane Burnet, Austrian Nobel prizewinner for work in immunology, has stated that there could be up to 100,000 cells in the body becoming cancerous each day, but that the average person's immune system effectively destroys these cancer cells. It is therefore important to stop negative thoughts about 'catching' cancer and concentrating on a positive approach, imagining your immune system working effectively and eliminating cancerous cells.

# Heart Disease

Fear of heart disease comes a close second to cancer phobia. And as we know fear can produce the symptoms of illness. Fear makes the heart beat faster and tension causes pains in the chest and other muscles so that someone feeling a pain in the muscles of the left arm, for instance, 'knows' he is on the way to a heart attack. If there is a history of heart trouble in the family, this can make things even worse. Many suspected heart attacks turn out to be acute anxiety attacks, much to the relief but embarrassment of the patient – embarrassed because she feels the doctors will consider her a nuisance.

Claire Weekes makes an important statement in her book, *Self Help for Your Nerves*, when she notes that: '*Heart pain proper is not felt in the heart.*' The soreness and pain you feel are merely muscular chest-wall strain, brought on by tension. You are aware of your heart beating and are drawing more attention to it by worrying. If you have been assured by your doctor that there is nothing wrong with your heart, you'll have to accept that it sometimes plays tricks on you – most likely due to your over-sensitive nerves. That constantly fast-beating, thumping, banging, shaking heart that seems to act up on you every day cannot harm you.

Isaac Marks tells of a patient who was so afraid that he might die of a heart attack, his doctor instructed him to try as hard as possible to make his heart beat faster and die of a heart attack right on the spot. He laughed and replied, 'Doc, I am trying hard but I can't do it.' He was instructed to go ahead and try to die from a heart attack each time his anticipatory anxiety troubled him. As he started laughing about his neurotic symptoms, he was able to distance himself from his neurosis.

The patient was instructed to try to die of a heart attack at least three times a day. The moment he started laughing at his symptoms and became willing to produce them intentionally, he changed his attitude towards his fear and it improved.

# Diabetes

Diabetes is yet another disease which frightens many people to the point of disrupting their lives. Merely being asked to produce a standard urine sample by the doctor can result in soaring anxiety. Posters which warn about the consequences of diabetes don't help. Amputation, blindness, kidney disease, they say. The phobic imagination works overtime!

Remember what I said about fear of the unknown? Marilyn contacted PAX last year hoping that she could help others by telling her story:

> My diabetes phobia was haunting me day and night and I was dreading going into hospital for a minor operation, not because of the operation itself but I knew it meant a thorough health check – and a urine sample.
>
> A few days later my doctor told me I was perfectly fit . . . apart

from a slightly raised blood sugar level. This was the news I had been dreading. I knew what it meant and I decided to see a consultant privately because I couldn't face a two-week wait for an NHS appointment.

The consultation was a nightmare and it ended with the knowledge that I *was* slightly diabetic. I was referred to the diabetic clinic at the NHS hospital and it was there that my phobia disappeared! The kind and understanding staff made it so easy. I attended lectures, watched videos and learned all about the disease. It suddenly wasn't frightening any more. I found out that it can be controlled and in my own case I just had to take two tablets a day and watch my diet.

It may sound ridiculous to say that becoming a diabetic was the best thing that happened to me but it has changed my life. The only slight reminder that remains of my phobia is that if I don't check my blood sugar level every day I start to worry, my imagination works overtime and I think, *Supposing it has increased; what if it is out of control?* I know that I have to face the problem and that avoidance could even lead me back into the miseries of a phobic state once more.

Ironically, developing the disease she feared most brought Marilyn an understanding of it that enabled her to overcome her phobia.

## Sex Disease Phobias

For centuries, the spectre of venereal disease hung over the population and syphilophobia, the fear of syphilis, was almost as serious as the disease itself. With the advent of antibiotics the phobia gradually faded.

The virginal bachelors who were susceptible to phobias about venereal diseases in the past – even though they had no sex life – are now being replaced by AIDS phobics, few of whom are ever likely to contract AIDS because they are so frightened they avoid sexual contact altogether. (AIDS is not, of course, specifically a sex disease, but sexual contact is one of the principal ways in which it is transmitted.) However, AIDS phobics feel that even celibacy is not going to protect them against the disease as long as there are others around who are HIV-positive and might pass it on. As one phobic explains:

I feel that we are not getting true information about how AIDS is passed from person to person. I know we are told that the virus cannot live in the open air and can only be passed by sexual contact, but I cannot now go into a public toilet; I dare not go to the dentist and there is no way I would have any sort of injection.

There is a simple test for AIDS, and that is the only way you'll find out whether or not you have it. The government provides detailed information that explains how the disease can be spread and identifies 'high risk' groups. You can consider yourself not at risk if you are, for instance, a middle-aged, married woman who has only had one partner (and whose partner has only had one partner), no blood transfusions or drug-taking habits.

Before fears of AIDS become full-blown phobias, I would advise anyone to contact one of the AIDS support organizations, such as the Terence Higgins Trust (see page 206), who will readily provide advice and information. As with all fears of disease, knowledge and understanding can prevent a phobia from developing.

## Smoking Phobia

Every era has its fashionable fears. These days the medical profession employs the media and the advertising companies to get their message across.

We all know that smoking damages our health, that heart disease and lung cancer and many respiratory disorders are a direct result of years of cigarette smoking. The dire warnings that have been hammered into us have resulted in many nervous people developing phobias about smoking.

Heavy smokers? Not likely. Most smokers seem oblivious to the hazards and continue to puff away unconcerned. The fact is that smoking phobias usually occur among people who don't smoke at all but are terrified of the effects of so-called 'passive smoking'.

One sufferer wrote to say that she will not allow smoking in her house – or in her garden. She has given up all her social activities, and will not go to anyone else's home in case somebody lights up. Although not specifically agoraphobic she is leaving her house less and less. She can see what is happening to her and is at a loss to know how to tackle it. In her letter she noted:

> I think it started when I watched a self-hypnosis video with a friend who wanted to stop smoking. I have never smoked but others smoking did not worry me. The film started with a pile of smouldering cigarette ends in an ashtray. A jug of water was poured into the ashtray and I could almost smell the disgusting smoking mess. Listening to the dire warnings and realizing just what smoking could do to the body really triggered off my phobia.
>
> Another thing that upsets me is that I used to love watching old black-and-white movies on afternoon television. These were the films I enjoyed in my youth. But everyone is smoking – passing silver cigarette cases to one another; snapping lighters in the middle of a love scene; blowing smoke into each other's faces. I cannot bear to watch now.

Another smoking phobic worked in an office where there were several smokers. She wrote to say:

> They just laughed when I asked them if they realized the dangers of smoking and how I, a passive smoker, was almost as much at risk as they were. I couldn't sleep for worrying about my health. Even if I changed my job I was likely to have to work with other smokers.
>
> One day I felt so bad I really thought I was going to die. I coughed and choked and couldn't breathe properly. A woman colleague drove me to the hospital and was very sympathetic, saying how selfish smokers can be.
>
> I thought at the very least I was suffering from some sort of asthma attack but do you know what they told me in the casualty department? Hyperventilation. They said I'd worked myself into a state by worrying about the cigarette smoke. I had to leave my job as even my friend turned against me and said I was a neurotic troublemaker.

As more and more firms are banning smoking, and there are fewer public places where it is allowed, so the threat of passive smoking will lessen. In the meantime, avoid the company of smokers if you must, and do seek help for any overwhelming, irrational fears.

## Fear of Doctors, Hospitals and Medical Procedures

Fifty PAX contacts with a fear of hospitals were asked, 'What is behind your fear?' None of those questioned were suffering from any condition that needed an operation, injections or any other form of treatment. So where did the fear come from? 'It's the atmosphere of the place', 'The smell of antiseptic', 'Seeing all those sick people makes me feel nervous', were just some of the responses. And they are all pretty vague. The negative image of a hospital seems to indicate that they find it a place you go to be told that you actually suffer from an illness, not somewhere you go to be cured.

The general hustle of a hospital – doctors and nurses, ambulances rushing to the casualty department, patients on trolleys – is overwhelming for the anxiety sufferer, and form the basis for the phobia, along with some of the less general fears noted above.

Although fears of blood, injections, anaesthetics and painful treatments are understandable, apparatus to test blood pressure or heart activity, for instance, is also often viewed with alarm and can even trigger a panic attack. In these cases it is not the procedure itself that is fear provoking but what alarming information it is going to produce. A hospital phobic wrote to tell of his fears:

> I have high blood pressure and have to have medication for it. Each month I saw my doctor and each month when he took my blood pressure I would beg him *not* to tell me what it was. Eventually, he insisted on telling me, saying I would be able to cope much better with my fears if I faced up to them. Although it was very high I did find that I was less bothered about it and could do something positive, such as taking more exercise and learning to relax properly instead of sitting and brooding.

Opticians, too, have their share of nervous patients who can not tolerate the apparatus used to test their eyesight. Often it is the well-known claustrophobic feeling of being trapped in a dark room – and there is also the underlying anticipation of being told that they have some serious eye disorder.

The best way to overcome these types of phobias is by gradual exposure, and discussing your concerns with a sympathetic doctor, optician or other member of the medical profession. See page 162 for more detailed steps to cope with your anxiety.

## Dentists

We could fill a whole chapter on dental phobia and luckily much more attention is being paid to patients' fears in these enlightened days. So often dental phobia is acute anticipatory anxiety. As we have seen, anxiety sufferers cannot tolerate the tension that builds up when waiting for something to happen. As children they could not play games such as hide-and-seek because they could not bear the tension while waiting to be found. Often they would emerge from their hiding place and give themselves up rather than have to wait any longer.

The days spent waiting for a dental appointment go slowly and when the time arrives to go to the surgery the patient has worked herself up into a dreadful state. The Relaxation for Living Foundation has produced a pamphlet called 'Don't Dread the Dentist'. Their first point is that you don't have to go to the dentist unless you really want to. Nobody is going to force you to go and until the time comes when you feel ready, there is no point in worrying about it in advance.

If you have decided to be very brave, or if you have toothache so agonizing that you will do *anything* to get rid of it, you will soon find that dentists today are by no means the ogres you expect them to be. The old view that most dentists really don't understand how anxious or phobic people feel, is entirely incorrect and outdated. Now that dentists are allowed to advertise I suggest you take a look through the Yellow Pages: 'Immediate evening appointments for nervous patients whenever possible'; 'Home visits for elderly or anxious patients'; 'Pleasant, relaxing environment'; 'Intravenous sedation for nervous patients'; 'We'll make you smile'; 'Anxious patients welcome!'; and

'Special facilities for nervous or anxious patients including intravenous anaesthetic/sedation/hypnosis' are only some of the dozens of similar advertisements in my area directory.

Perhaps you have a fear of anaesthetics? Some of us who lived through the war remember that black smelly rubber mask and the sickly-sweet smell of the gas. Your phobia may have kept you away from a dental surgery for the last thirty years. Admittedly, a fear of hypodermic needles can cause problems here, though gums can be treated with a local anaesthetic before an injection these days.

The examination itself before treatment can be equally alarming as the dental surgeon taps his way round your teeth, muttering to his assistant. He is only counting teeth and making notes, not about to practise some refined torture you have never heard of in your unsuspecting mouth. A number of dentists have abandoned this preliminary mapping out of your mouth and leave that until the pressing necessity of treatment has been dealt with, by which time you are so relieved you don't mind the tooth count and check.

Is it the dentist's chair that bothers you? The old-style chair in which you started by sitting bolt upright until it was cranked backwards was bad enough, but the modern chair is more like an operating table and its very shape can strike fear into the heart. Lying down with your head virtually in the dentist's lap and your feet pointing towards the ceiling can make you feel very vulnerable and trapped. An understanding dentist will help you to overcome any aversion to the chair and many will start treatment with the patient sitting upright on an ordinary chair, gradually transferring to the treatment couch when he or she is accustomed to being horizontal and her general fears have subsided.

In their pamphlet 'Don't Dread the Dentist', Relaxation for Living offer the following tips to overcome a dentist phobia:

• If you are having an injection, relax as deeply as possible, breathe in as the needle approaches your mouth and breathe out as the needle goes in. This way, you probably won't feel it
• Continue to keep your attention away from the work being

done. As well as concentrating on something at a distance, bring your thoughts to your muscles every few minutes for a quick check that you are still relaxed

● Check that your jaw is loose, your forehead smooth, your shoulders dropped, your hands unclenched. Be sure that your head and the whole length of your body are resting heavily in the chair. Make certain that your legs are flopped outwards and your toes uncurled

● See that your breathing is gentle and smooth, low down in your tummy. If it is not, then encourage it to be so

● There is so much for you to take charge of in the dentist's chair, the time passes faster than you expect! Never forget that he is able to work more quickly and with greater care and accuracy when you are calm and relaxed. Also remember that a relaxed body actually feels pain far less than does one that is tensed up. (A cassette on dental phobia is now available from PAX.)

## Face Your Fear

Before you can start to overcome your phobia you have to look at it and then admit what it is and what you are going to do about it. If you can not bear to look at the word *cancer*, take a deep breath and write it down on a piece of paper. Not once but twenty, a hundred times. It is just a word and has no meaning out of context.

This may appear to be a pretty useless exercise but only someone who has such a severe phobia can appreciate how difficult it might be to admit to the fear of a word. For those who think they can face learning more about the phobic illness, *don't* turn to a medical encyclopaedia as this could do more harm than good. You can get reassurance and advice from the various Health Call telephone lines, from magazines and from the associations connected with the illness, which have their own self-help groups.

Hypnotherapy has proved particularly helpful in the treatment of illness phobias, the patient learning to understand the problem while in a completely relaxed state.

On the whole, I feel that some form of behaviour therapy

with supportive psychotherapy is the best approach to all illness phobias.

Any medical condition, any medical or dental procedure, any part of the body, and somewhere in the world there is probably someone who has a phobia about them.

Here are two final examples of phobias about parts of the body. Although they are not illness phobias, they are extremely debilitating, and very real to the sufferer:

I feel permanently light-headed . . . I mean literally. I have the sensation that my head is the weight of a balloon and could easily be dislodged and just float away.

Another PAX member has the opposite problem:

I was watching a programme on television when it was mentioned that the average head weighed twenty pounds or more. I have become obsessed with this. I weighed out twenty pounds of potatoes and was horrified to feel just how heavy they were. Surely my neck isn't strong enough to hold up such a heavy object as my head?

Now I can not get this idea out of my mind. I can not sit up straight and hold my head up without a surgical collar, and the more I think about it the heavier my head feels. My doctor assures me that obsessional thoughts gradually wear off and I hope that one day I will be able to behave normally again. At present I am only really comfortable when I am lying down.

Whatever your phobia and however peculiar it may seem to other people you can do something to help yourself using the techniques we've discussed. Don't worry about what others may think of you!

# 12

# OBSESSIVE-COMPULSIVE DISORDER

About two per cent of the population suffer from obsessive-compulsive disorder. The condition is far less common than panic disorder and both sexes are affected equally. In *Phobia: The Facts*, Dr Goodwin defines the individual with an obsessional personality as:

> . . . punctual, ordered, scrupulous, meticulous and dependable. He is also rigid, stubborn, pedantic and something of a bore. He has trouble making up his mind, but once made up is single-minded and obstinate. Many individuals with obsessive-compulsive disorder have obsessional personalities ante-dating the illness.

And in *Living With Fear*, Professor Isaac Marks writes:

> Both obsessive thoughts and compulsive rituals tend to occur more in people who have always had meticulous and perfectionist personalities, though such problems can occur in the most slipshod of individuals.

'What do you think of these definitions?' I asked a group of people at a self-help group for obsessive-compulsive disorder. I thought they would feel rather insulted, but they all agreed that the doctors' descriptions were pretty accurate – though the men in particular drew the line at being described as a bit of a bore!

So what *is* obsessive compulsive disorder? Obsessions are persistent and distressing unwanted thoughts or impulses. Compulsions are acts resulting from obsessions. The obsessive person desperately tries to resist the obsession and put it out of his or her mind.

Formerly, the advice was to crowd out undesirable thoughts by replacing them with positive and pleasant ones, but this makes sufferers even more agitated and the effort to try and think positive becomes an equal obsession.

At the end of the day it is hardly surprising that the anxious person is exhausted with the effort of trying to cope. Suffering from 'brain fatigue', their thinking becomes distorted, as repetitive and compulsive thoughts whiz round and round in their heads, driving them to distraction.

It would be difficult to find anyone in the world who was not mildly superstitious in some way, or who did not practise an occasional harmless ritual. Many people carry a talisman with them: a St Christopher charm, for instance, or other 'lucky' object. We 'touch wood', following a boastful or hopeful remark (touching the sacred oak to placate the god Thor), cross our fingers for luck (an early Christian act of making the sign of the cross), or say 'Bless you' when someone sneezes (because traditionally, it was believed that the spirit was in danger at that vulnerable moment.

In *Manwatching*, Desmond Morris writes:

From the beginning of time man has been perpetually occupied with the business of inventing curious, magical acts of self-defence. These all consist of some activity which, if performed, is supposed to prevent bad luck in the future. The fact that there is never any logical connection between the act and the outcome does nothing to deter the superstitious. They continue to protect themselves by cautiously performing the acts, 'just in case'.

Anxious people are particularly addicted to superstitious practices. Not, perhaps, the ones such as avoiding ladders on the pavement, throwing salt over their shoulder, or staying in bed on Friday 13, but the number of personalized protections with which they surround themselves is endless. At one end of the scale are those with full-blown obsessive neuroses who must have professional help to overcome their problems, but the rest of us have our own sets of rituals and 'soteria' that we rely on to keep us safe throughout the day. We have seen how this begins in childhood. The baby with his comfort blanket, the little girl who won't be parted from her doll or teddy bear, the way children will touch objects 'for luck'.

As we get older, particularly if we are prone to being anxious, we build up our own collections of superstitions – those magical protective acts of self-defence.

'If only I behave like this, do it that way, repeat this phrase in my mind, everything will be alright . . .' How many times have you used these criteria to try to impose an order on future events? We become locked into these patterns because we are afraid of what might happen if we deviate from them in the slightest way – we are afraid of uncertainty.

George has to drive once round the block each morning before continuing his journey to the office. Jessica, who is fourteen, has to murmur good luck 'spells' every day on the way to school. Another teenager has to listen to a particular song before he can face the day. He takes his Walkman to college in case there is a crisis, at which time he will find a quiet spot to play the song through again. Margaret gets out her patience cards and plays three games before breakfast. If the cards 'come out' she will have a lucky day.

Some years ago an agoraphobic member of the Open Door invented 'Aggie Phobie', a mythical sufferer who always wore dark glasses when she went out, pushed a shopping trolley and carried a packet of strong peppermints. Only with these props was she able to get out and about. This character was immediately recognizable to almost every agoraphobia sufferer, and she has appeared in many books and been referred to by doctors and psychiatrists.

'This could be me,' exclaimed new contacts in The Open Door and PAX. Over the years, details of Aggie's lifestyle have been built up by fellow sufferers, based on their own experiences. Aggie's day might begin by getting out of bed – always on the same side – and she must put on her clothes in exactly the same sequence every morning. Her left shoe must go on before the right or 'something' might go wrong during the day. She must clean her teeth before washing her face, then prepare breakfast, making the toast before heating the kettle. She dreads the arrival of the postman in case he brings a letter that might upset her. She must kiss her partner as he leaves the house, murmuring the correct farewell: 'See you later'. Supposing she said 'Goodbye'; he might never return!

Anxious people need to feel that they are in control of a situation. The Aggie Phobie character is not suffering from a full-blown obsessive-compulsive disorder but she needs her personalized superstitions and rituals to help her feel 'safe'.

Aggie Phobie carries on these activities throughout her day, as we can see from her shopping expedition. Having set forth with her comforting props she will walk along the road, crossing at specific points – and crossing back again to avoid her 'black spots'; for instance, a tall building or a blank wall. She will then visit the shops in the prescribed sequence. To see an ambulance or pass an undertaker's establishment reminds her to mutter a protective word or phrase that she may have learnt originally in the school playground. Any sort of upset or unexpected incident – bad news about a neighbour, a road accident, a passer-by in distress – will throw our Aggie into a state of upset, causing her to scurry home before panicky feelings overwhelm her.

With her family safely home and fed, Aggie can put up her feet and relax . . . except that she will then start to worry about the next day. And, of course, there is the bedtime ritual to get through.

A man who is struggling to control anxiety will catch a particular train to work, drive by a certain fixed route, buy his regular newspaper and pray that there will be no unscheduled stops, traffic jams or unusual occurrences. He may plan his lunch hour – a nearby pub or, better still, sandwiches so that he does not have to go out at all. His office must run like clockwork, and woe betide anyone who upsets his schedule. And so it goes on.

Rituals are common to both phobic people and those suffering from obsessive-compulsive disorder. In the latter, however, they become much more than just harmless rituals. Obsessive-compulsive disorder is a chronic or recurring illness *dominated by* obsessions and compulsions. It is usually more difficult to treat than a phobia.

Isaac Marks says that treatment follows similar principles to those used in treating phobias, but it can take longer because the ramifications can be so much more extensive in the sufferer's life.

## Obsessional Rituals

These are compulsions, or repetitive acts of washing, counting, checking (*Did I leave the fire on?*), cleaning and/or touching objects. Compulsions are inseparable from the obsessions from which they arise. A compulsion is an obsession expressed as an action.

Peter, a self-employed man in his forties, told me that his bedtime ritual lasted four hours. He had to check doors, locks, switches and taps in strict order, and if he missed something he had to start from the beginning again. His written list ran into eight pages. We decided that he would pick one obvious task that could not possibly be dangerous left undone, and remove it from his list. We decided that he would leave the oven door open deliberately one night. This caused him great agitation but he did it and by the end of the week he had crossed this off his list.

Peter then decided he would seek professional help, having avoided it in the past because he was embarrassed by the problem. He was afraid his GP would not be cooperative and was relieved to find that his compulsions were treated seriously. He is now on an NHS waiting list for treatment but is getting support from his doctor for the time being.

Behaviour therapy is the most promising solution for obsessive-compulsive disorder, though improvement is slow and often some form of supportive psychotherapy is necessary to deal with underlying anxieties. That out-of-control imagination is working overtime where obsessional ideas, thoughts and pictures are concerned. Upsetting visions of murder, rape or accidents concerning the sufferers' nearest and dearest become impossible to shift and cause great distress.

Claire Weekes, in *Self Help for Your Nerves*, is as reassuring as ever:

> The tired mind seems to lose resilience so that frightening thoughts may seem to cling tenaciously. The bewildered sufferer often makes the mistake of trying to push away unwelcome thoughts or replace them with other thoughts. The more he fights in this way, the tenser he becomes and the more stubbornly thoughts seem to cling . . . Small wonder he despairs as he tries to find ways to keep unwanted thoughts at bay.

Dr Weekes explains that it is not the compulsion itself that is frightening – for example, repeating a phrase or humming a tune endlessly – but the *feeling* of being obliged to do it. If you can accept the fact that these thoughts and urges will keep coming, and that you don't have to fight them all the time, they will gradually lose the power to worry you and you won't be so exhausted and frightened.

## Obsessional Fears

These fears are often of dirt, germs, contamination, and of potential weapons such as knives and scissors. Very often there is no rationale behind the fear, simply an inexplicable abhorrence for the object in question.

Daphne, a mother of four and a freelance writer, feels she would rather keep her problem under control herself and does not want to seek therapy:

> I have a horror of knives pointing towards me and even a finger pointed at me makes me recoil. I think that it is going to stick in my eye. I have to keep all knives in a drawer. I can handle them myself but my family have firm instructions at meal times to hold their knives low and pointing away from me where possible.

While Daphne has her own obsessional fears under control, they are still an everyday issue in her life, and therefore disruptive. Like other aspects of obsessive-compulsive disorders, the best treatment comes from trained therapists and analysts, who will treat the fear that lies behind the obsession.

The most common compulsive ritual is constant washing. Behind this lies a fear of germs and contamination and frequently there is a history of adult over-insistence on cleanliness and threats of lurking germs just waiting to cause disease. Compulsive washing is enormously time-consuming. Some people will wash dozens of times a day, particularly after touching something – anything at all.

Mandy's parents insisted that she had treatment privately. At eighteen she was unable to leave the house because of her obsession with cleanliness. She wrote to the PAX newsletter to say:

> Since having behaviour therapy I am much better and don't feel the need to wash quite so often, though the urge is still there below the surface. Before treatment I had to scrub my hands dozens of times a day until the skin was raw and bleeding.

Sometimes, the underlying anxiety may subside – even burn itself out – and sufferers find themselves able to tackle and overcome their disorders. Dorothy is one of the lucky ones:

> Do you pray when you have to do something that frightens you? I found that I *had* to pray automatically every ten minutes or so. Please, God, let me feel all right; please, God, make me able to go to the shop, talk to the woman next door, get through the day without a panic attack. One day recently, I read something that made me stop and think. I wasn't really communicating with the Almighty, but repeating a protective phrase that had no meaning. God wants me to stand on my own feet, I told myself. I mustn't keep asking him for favours but make positive statements to myself. I *will* feel all right. I *can* go to the shop . . . and if I don't manage it this time, or if I have a bad day, next time it will be easier.
>
> Now I pray for others who are in trouble, or for my nearest and dearest. I know that God *is* helping me. I don't need to keep asking but now get on with my life and try to rely on myself.

Don't hesitate to ask your doctor to refer you to a psychiatrist or psychologist – they are aware that obsessive-compulsive disorder can be a serious problem and will be able to help. In the meantime, here are a few suggestions about what you might do to help you face up to those fears:

- Think through your average day from the moment you wake up in the morning. Make a list of your own particular compulsions and protective thoughts – you will be surprised how long it is.
- When you actually study the written list you will find that they begin to lose their grip on you.
- One step at a time, gradually tackle the habits; for instance, put your right shoe on before the left, go to a different shop and walk there by a different route. It is the little victories that are important.

Soon you'll find yourself progressing further and further from your obsessive-compulsive state.

## Self-Help Groups

These are gradually beginning to appear on the scene and though at present they are mainly in the London area, it is to be hoped that they will soon spread to other parts of the country. For up-to-date details of some of these groups, please contact PAX (see page 202 for details).

# 13
# SOCIAL FEARS AND PHOBIAS

A social phobia is basically a fear of being looked at, of performing any sort of action or of drawing attention to oneself in any way. The sufferer is afraid of being embarrassed by making a mistake or making a fool of himself. Unlike most other phobias which are more common in women, social phobias tend to affect the sexes equally. At the root of the sufferer's embarrassment is a fear of losing control in some way or not being able to continue what he is doing while he is being watched.

Most social phobias occur in adolescence or in the early twenties. A sensitive youngster lacking confidence – and/or with a poor self-image through being overweight or spotty – might develop a fear of eating in public, of being ridiculed, or of blushing in front of other people.

Of course most of us go through periods, particularly in our teens, when we feel like this but we survive and in a few years we can look back at the lessons we learned whilst coming to terms with life. In retrospect it's easy to feel sympathy for the confused youngsters we once were. Unfortunately, others find that their fears take over and unless they receive help in overcoming them, they may develop into phobias.

Sufferers from social phobias often find themselves unable to relate to other people on any sort of personal level. They have difficulty expressing their emotions and feel that they can not get close to others physically or emotionally. Often they are only children who have had an over-protected social upbringing and have not developed a sense of independence, and are therefore unable to function adequately in an adult social world.

One can see that if school phobia persists and is not treated, it may develop into a serious social phobia and chronic agora-phobia. An adolescent agoraphobe is in a sorry plight, particularly if he or she becomes housebound. Lack of contact with other teenagers may result in the phobic adolescent retreating into day-dreams and fantasies, avoiding contact with the real world outside his or her home and inevitably losing touch with other people. A female adolescent may hope for a romantic hero to arrive at her front door and sweep her off her feet, though she certainly would not be able to cope if he wanted to take her away from her home.

It is especially difficult to persuade adolescents to take part in any treatment programme as recovery would mean having to face up to the realities of normal everyday life.

Some older women who have become housebound may focus all their emotions on to a well-known celebrity – often a pop singer, and usually dead (safer). Recently, there was a television documentary about a woman who was 'in love' with Elvis Presley, and her restricted lifestyle revolved around the singer, his records and a mountain of other memorabilia. And becoming housebound can affect people of any age. Becoming a complete recluse at an age as young as twenty two is a tragedy. Philip lives on his own in a bedsit, so ashamed of his fears that he has broken off all contact with his parents. He leaves his bedsit only to see his doctor and arrange for his invalidity benefit. The only food he eats are pizzas, which are delivered to his door when he telephones from a pay phone in the hall downstairs. When he runs out of money he doesn't eat. He did have a special pizza for his Christmas dinner last year but having indulged in this expense he went without for the rest of the holiday.

Social phobics have a fear of groups of people and this is one of the situations where social phobia and agoraphobia tend to overlap – although the experts insist that they are quite separate. In a crowd, the agoraphobe will feel the need to escape. She feels trapped by her inability to detach herself quickly from the situation and she will escape back to her home as soon as possible.

The social phobic person has not the same need to escape

from a situation – it is people she fears. She can not bear to be looked at, to have her body space invaded, to be touched, even inadvertently. Some sufferers find it physically impossible to touch or be touched by anyone other than members of their own immediate family.

Social phobias do not evoke much sympathy in those who have never experienced them. On the whole, they seem very trivial and sufferers do their best to hide them, knowing they will probably be laughed at. Walking past a line of people, standing at a bank counter writing a cheque, speaking in front of a class: such simple actions for most of us, but agonizing for many phobic sufferers. I received a letter from a man telling me about the problem he has writing in front of another person. His writing, in the letter, was perfectly legible but he enclosed a sample of writing he had tried to do with someone looking over his shoulder and it was impossible to read the spidery scrawl. 'My hand becomes sweaty and shakes so much I can barely hold a pen,' he told me in his letter. 'I have a perfectly good job in an office but I go out of my way to avoid even signing my name if someone is near.'

How can a visit to the bank be as traumatic as a visit to a dentist? It is the way a phobic person's mind works, always jumping ahead, expecting the worst. One social phobic explains his fear of visiting the bank, the panic that rushes through his mind:

> There are a lot of people waiting; I feel trapped already. I should have checked how much there is in my account. Supposing there isn't enough to cover the cheque? Why is the bank clerk looking at me in that funny way? What is the computer telling her? Why has she walked away? Everyone is looking at me.

By this time, he can hardly take the money because his hand is shaking so much.

Another common problem is a fear of blushing. As with every other phobia, it is difficult for a non-sufferer to understand just how distressing this can be. Even a delicate and flattering flush sends out warnings to the blusher that she – it is usually, but not always, a woman – is making herself obvious and that everyone is looking at her.

A sixteen year old told me:

> I cannot sit opposite another passenger in a bus or train. I feel this awful heat sneaking up my neck and all over my face, causing me to hyperventilate, and I start to feel panicky as I just *know* that everyone is looking at me. I am told that there is little change in my colour when this happens but the only way I can feel comfortable is to wear very heavy make-up with a green tinge. This is the advice I received from a magazine agony aunt. I have convinced myself this really does hide the 'rosy glow', as my boyfriend calls it.

Another teenage girl wrote,

> I cannot bear to be looked at. I am afraid I might do something silly, make a fool of myself, make a mistake or lose control in some way. More than anything I am afraid of anyone *knowing* I'm afraid.

Once again, this girl's problem is the need to escape before she commits the dreadful crime of drawing attention to herself. As we have seen, this is closely linked to the agoraphobic state. Avoiding social situations means that she may become housebound, but unlike true agoraphobia – where she can find sanctuary from her fears in her home – the social phobia sufferer finds that her problems follow her.

To this person the arrival of an unexpected caller can be a disaster. The sound of the doorbell, a knock on the door sets off warning signals. Who is it? Why are they here? What do they want? These thoughts flash through her mind as she ducks into a corner of the hall where she can not be seen. Her heart races, her mouth dries up as she feels the situation is getting out of hand and she won't be able to cope. The only thing to do is to stay hidden until they go away. Unfortunately, there are times when such visitors must be faced.

Even the telephone can be as alarming as the unexpected caller at the door. How can a telephone bell strike fear into someone's heart? Firstly, when you are hypersensitive, the sudden sound can make you jump and your heart beat faster.

Then there is the question, who is on the other end of the line? If fear has dried your mouth, it is difficult to speak. When you are over-breathing your voice sounds strange even to yourself and you worry about what the caller might think. Will you be able to answer their questions? Can you make an excuse to put the phone down? You have to answer it because it may be a member of the family in trouble or some other emergency (the 'what if' syndrome again).

But suppose it is someone you really don't want to speak to and you can not terminate the conversation. Once again, it is the feeling of being trapped that is upsetting.

Another very common fear is of eating in public. It may be a dislike of having to eat and drink in front of other people, or it could be bound up with feelings of being trapped at a table in the middle of a restaurant.

It is difficult enough to eat in public when your mouth is dry, your hands are shaking and a constricted throat makes it almost impossible to swallow. The sufferer feels that their constant nervous gulping will cause comment from others at the table. It is interesting to see that this may be quite a short-lived problem. It can strike quite suddenly, as it did when my husband was studying for his law exams. Official dinners and even dinner for two in a cosy restaurant were out of the question as he could not sit through a meal without feeling ill and panicky. Luckily the problem lasted only two years and has never returned.

## SITUATIONAL PHOBIAS

What is a situational phobia? These are fears that occur in specific places or situations and are only loosely intertwined with the original understanding of the phobia.

Apprehension, anxiety and panic attacks can happen *any-where* – in an open field or on the motorway, when walking in the street or travelling in a bus or train. They can take place at work, in school, in a shop, church, theatre and even in the home. As we discussed earlier, it is not the situation itself that the phobic person fears but it is the feelings that occur in that situation. Avoid the situation and you avoid the fear. But in the end that just makes things worse.

The experts feel that social phobias and agoraphobia are different, but they are, in fact, very closely linked. Most agoraphobes have multiple fears – many of which could come under the heading of social phobias – but the common denominator is the fear of being trapped in a situation from which there is no immediate escape. Like eating in public, for instance.

## Self Help for Social and Situational Phobics

Liz belonged to a self-help group. It took her a long time to decide that she would join because she was uneasy with other people, thinking that they were looking at her and making remarks about her behind her back. As she became used to the other members she confided that her worst fear was of eating in public; she was anxious to overcome this and other members were keen to help. Boosted by their enthusiasm Liz's self-confidence improved until she was able to face the first step. Here are the steps she undertook to get over her fears. Perhaps you can come up with a version of this that will help you overcome your own individual fears.

● Mary suggested that a small teashop in the town could be the first place to experiment. Morning coffee when the place was virtually empty and just the two of them at a corner table. Liz got as far as the teashop, but on the first occasion was not able to venture inside. She and Mary watched other people come and go while she nibbled a chocolate wafer biscuit that Mary had provided. Luckily, Liz had a sense of humour and could see the funny side of the situation – she was eating in front of another person and that was all that mattered.

● Mary took Liz to the teashop on several occasions. They walked up and down together outside; then Liz was persuaded to cross the threshold and stay inside for a brief moment.

● On the next occasion, Mary sat at a table and ordered two cups of coffee. Liz managed to sit with her for a few moments before returning to the car, which was parked outside the shop.

The second time they practised this exercise Liz managed to sip some coffee, then leave the table for a few minutes, walking around outside then returning to finish the coffee.

● Now other members of the group joined Liz and Mary for morning coffee and eventually, when she had got over her fear of eating in front of her friends she progressed to dining out at a restaurant with her husband.

Reading this account you might think that this was achieved in a short time, but in fact it took several weeks before Liz felt at all comfortable in the situation. This is just an example of how one woman faced her fear of eating in front of other people. If you want to tackle your problem constructively you must develop a plan for your recovery. After all, no one would build a house without a detailed drawing or go on a long journey without a map. Here are a few self-help tips:

● Buy a notebook and plot your way to a normal life. You may not be used to writing things down, particularly if you have never kept a diary or put your thoughts on paper, but this is important. You can't possibly chart your recovery if you haven't something concrete to help you. To see things written down in black and white is important and even more so to be able to look back at what you have written and actually see the progress you have made.

● Write down what you would do if you were free of your anxieties. List the reasons you have for wanting to recover – specific reasons, not just woolly remarks like 'I want to feel better'.

● Write down 'How My Life Would Be Changed', and think of a list of ten things you would be able to do that you cannot do at present.

The results from three different people might look like this. Sufferer number one – married with three children:

I could handle attacks of panic in the home;

I could stay indoors on my own, answer the door or tele-
phone;
I would be able to relax;
I could talk to visitors who come to my house;
I could walk round the garden;
I could go shopping with my family;
I could visit friends; and
I could go on holiday with my family.

Writing these points down should make you feel more in
control of the situation. Here are some more.

Sufferer number two is male, and in a responsible position at
work:

I could go to work on public transport without feeling
panicky;
I could attend meetings and sit in someone else's office;
I could fly on holiday with my partner;
I could attend business lunches; and
I could accept promotion without worrying whether I could
handle the responsibility.

The final sufferer is a fourteen-year-old girl:

I could travel to school without feeling anxious;
I wouldn't have nightmares about school;
I could concentrate on my school work;
I could go into Assembly and stay there;
I would feel at ease in the classroom;
I could enjoy shopping with my friends; and
I could enjoy social events.

Not complete lists by any means but enough to show the
enormous differences between anxiety sufferers and why it is
so difficult for those who haven't suffered to understand. Here
are some further steps to consider:

179

• Complete your list, then *try to feel enthusiastic about it*. You have got to get your imagination under control and instead of letting it depress you, make it work for you

• Try to see yourself doing these things free from fear. Of course it is going to be difficult and instead of vaguely thinking about recovery, start to tackle it a little bit at a time

• Attempt some creative visualization. Take just one of your worrying problems and break it down into tiny progressive steps. Write it down or you will never remember the steps.

Let's take the fourteen-year-old sufferer as an example. While she sits at home trying to concentrate on her homework, her mind keeps skipping ahead to the next day when she has to walk to the bus, sit through assembly, and face crowds of noisy children. Too much rush and movement, too much noise, too much tension.

When Jenny goes to bed she should concentrate on breathing correctly to help her calm down and relax, instead of letting her mind range haphazardly over her fears. She should think about breakfast the next morning, see herself chatting to her family in a relaxed mood, imagine the walk to the bus stop and getting on the bus, meeting her friends, walking into the classroom, and going into assembly. While she is doing this she must visualize the situations as normal – enjoyable, if possible! But most of all she must visualize the sequence of events as *non-threatening*.

I don't mean that Jenny should try and think about all these things in one night. Perhaps she should get as far as imagining the walk to the bus stop and doing this for several nights before going further.

Our first sufferer might visualize herself walking around her empty house when her family has gone for the day. She should go into each room and stay there for a few minutes, breathing correctly whilst telling herself that she feels relaxed and calm.

Our businessman is going to think about getting to his office, arriving there relaxed because he has not been hyperventilating, making himself a cup of coffee and looking forward to his day.

I know what it is like. I've been there and this technique does work, replacing the galloping terrors of anticipatory anxiety that can be so crippling.

# Step Two: Facing Your Fears

However successful you are with your breathing exercises, imagination practice and relaxation, you still have to face the fact that none of these will prevent sudden panic attacks. The important part of creative visualization is not necessarily that you will feel no panic when the event happens but that you do not suffer by living the occasion over and over again in advance.

The very term 'panic' suggests an overwhelming and uncontrollable sensation, but the fact is that with practice one can distance oneself from the feeling and even learn how to turn it off . . . Although many exposures to panic may be required, someone who experiences the feelings over and over again comes to understand eventually that it is not in itself damaging and sooner or later – usually sooner – every panic attack goes away.

But the typical phobia sufferer has been through panic attacks very many times in the past without getting used to the feeling and without coming to believe any such thing. Why should these new experiments lead to a different result?

THE DIFFERENCE LIES IN THE ATTITUDE WITH WHICH THE PHOBIC PERSON APPROACHES THE EXPERIENCE.

Usually she is intent only on getting away from the frightening situation as quickly as possible and pays no real attention to what is actually happening to her. When she approaches the phobic situation purposefully, however, with the willingness and even the intention of becoming panicky, she will gradually be able to master her feelings. It is a fundamentally different experience. Under such circumstances it is sometimes difficult to have a panic attack! The essential difference is, perhaps, as it is in other aspects of behaviour, between being active and being passive.

IT IS THE ACT OF MAKING SOMETHING HAPPEN RATHER THAN WAITING FOR IT TO HAPPEN.

# Step Three: Tackling the Problem

You have made a list of the things you are going to do. Now is the time to go into action. Let us consider first, not those who are housebound and starting from square one, but those people who are out in the world struggling to keep their anxieties under control. If you have to jump in at the deep end every day you obviously can not afford to practise thinking yourself into a panic attack just so that you can face it and work through it. I certainly could not have done that. But there are certain situations you can tackle. For instance:

● Go out with friends at lunchtime instead of eating sandwiches in the office

● Go to school half an hour earlier in the morning and wander around the buildings on your own, if at all possible

● Don't stick to the same routine throughout the day. Make yourself do something a little different so that you break your 'safe' pattern.

Every individual has their own particular set of problems and it would be impossible to try and list or even guess them all. It is up to you to study your situation.

● Carefully list the obstacles that must be overcome, however small and insignificant they may seem, because it is with these small steps that you approach the greater difficulties.

A success in one phobic situation makes coping in other places easier. If one dangerous place seems less frightening, so will all the others. The area in which the phobic person can live comfortably begins to expand, just as it shrank in the past when the condition was worsening. Although difficult, this process by which the sufferer learns to be unafraid is straightforward. The more time she stays in the phobic situation, the less frightening that situation becomes.

You failed today? So what? It doesn't matter. The important thing is that you took your first step by deciding to try. You are still playing the game. Whatever happens you must not get despondent and feel you have failed.

- Write down in your notebook, 'Today I have made the effort. Tomorrow I will succeed.'
- Tomorrow you will try a little harder, push yourself a little further and aim to record a success in your diary.

When you look back in a few weeks time you will be able to plot the progress you have made. I promise you that it will make you feel good!

## PANIC IN THE HOME

Why do some people have panic attacks in their homes? The one place where they should expect to feel safe can become as much a threat as a crowded Underground train. Whatever the original cause of your anxiety state, the phobia, the irrational fear, is the current problem. When panic strikes you feel that you are in an alien and dangerous situation – even if you are sitting in your own living room. You feel that something terrible is about to happen, that your mind and body are under such stress they cannot survive without cracking up.

It is *not knowing* that is so frightening, isn't it? Fear of the unknown and fear of the fear: the two greatest fears of all – fear of what *might* happen, not of what is actually happening to you at this moment.

So you feel terrible. What you are doing is projecting your thoughts and thinking that in the next few minutes you will feel even worse and that something frightful will happen. You can not imagine yourself ever feeling normal again. Because of this you may try and hang on to other people, seeing them as a lifeline to normality. You then get to the stage of thinking that you can not cope without this lifeline.

But you *can* manage without other people and you must learn to let go of them. You may say, 'I can't stay in the house on my own' but this negative remark will only increase the problem. The first thing you must learn to do is to face up to the problem in a different way. Tell yourself, 'I feel bad when I am left on my own but this does not mean I can't do it if I try.'

You are not really afraid of being alone . . . you are afraid of being left with yourself and your fears. You must practise staying with yourself for just five minutes – in a room apart from the family, initially – then staying in the house when everyone goes out. Get out that notebook and write down the length of time you lasted and aim to add another five minutes every few days.

You do need a cooperative partner or family to keep popping in and out of the house for increasingly long periods, but surely they will think it a worthwhile exercise? Aim at spending a couple of hours on your own with a telephone to hand and you will feel you are really on your way!

Many families are supportive but, again, people are funny and often don't want their nearest and dearest to know just how bad they feel. A pity, because if your partner, parents or children don't understand and are not prepared to try to be helpful you can sink even deeper into depression and despair, if you allow yourself to do so.

It is not always possible to find someone who will help you tackle your problem. It is pointless for self-help manuals to say that you must have another person to guide you if there is no one available or willing to help. There are circumstances in which there is only you, therefore you are the only person who can help yourself.

# 14
# SELF HELP – FOR EVERYONE

There are some people whose anxiety state is so severe that they feel there is nothing they can do to help themselves. Some can not go out, others can not be left in the house on their own. When someone has reached this stage they are certainly not in a position to take part in any structured therapeutic programme. They will give up trying to read and put into practice any self-help advice because they feel it would be impossible, they are not in a fit state; their minds are not working properly so they can not absorb instructions.

So where do you start?

First of all it is important that you are receiving proper medical care. Unfortunately, many people expect their doctor to 'make them better' quickly and the doctor, in many cases, can do nothing much else apart from prescribing drugs. Really severe cases of anxiety and depression that arise from anxiety may need a break in hospital, but don't start worrying about that! If you are not happy with your GP it is very simple these days to change to another, though I know that this can sometimes mean personal problems if you have been with your doctor for many years, or live in an area where it is not possible to find someone near you.

There are a number of tips that will help you to overcome your fears or phobias, and there is plenty of choice involved. The following should provide some helpful advice.

## Change Your Attitude to Life

You must realize when you plan to change your attitude to life that you are not going to change your anxious personality and become brave and outgoing; you will always remain a rather sensitive, perhaps nervous, person. But should you want to tackle your fears you will find life more pleasant as you gain confidence. Many, if not most of the creative people throughout the ages have suffered from emotional problems and even, in some cases, from severe mental illness. This is the price that often has to be paid for being born over-sensitive, imaginative and creative.

You are in good company with the world's great artists, writers, poets and musicians, many of whom have suffered in the same way. When you are feeling well enough you must consider what talents *you* may be hiding and learn to express your emotions through them.

## But Who Am I?

This is the question that many sufferers ask themselves. Much of the time they feel out of touch with the rest of the world. Do you feel like this? Do constant anxiety and panic attacks drag you down so that you feel unreal most of the time? Of course you are depressed, but you are quite likely to feel that way because of the possibility that nothing will ever change, that you will never feel any better, that no one understands, and that you are alone.

There is one person who can help. You. But perhaps you don't really know that person; you are frightened of yourself. When did you last take a look at your reflection in a mirror? Scary, isn't it? That person looking back at you doesn't seem to be anyone you know.

Of course you feel uneasy with other people. If you don't know yourself, how are you going to communicate with another person? There is a book called *Why Am I Afraid To Tell You Who I Am?*. Well, one answer might be, because I don't *know* who I am. The book says that the answer is, because this is all I have and if you don't like it I have nothing else. You have to learn to like yourself before you can expect anyone else to like you.

186

# Do-It-Yourself Therapies

What can you do in a situation when you are in a state of anxiety and depression? Sitting around feeling helpless is not going to help your recovery. However bad you feel there is *something* you can do. You may think you are not well enough to plan ahead, but try to make a list of the things you *can* do. If you have taken even the smallest step forward it will boost your morale.

'But I am in a constant state of panic,' you may say. 'Everything is unreal, I cannot think coherently. I am incapable of doing anything at all.'

*Rocking:* When you are feeling really low try rocking yourself backwards and forwards. You will have seen films of distressed refugees, survivors from disasters and those suffering from emotional traumas. When there is nothing they can do they sit on the ground and rock. Through the ages babies have been rocked in cradles and a child is soothed by the rhythmic movements when lulled in its mother's arms.

Rocking helps to relax the body and drain away tensions. No-one really knows just how this works but it seems likely that the rhythmic motion helps to counteract urgent messages which are being sent from the muscles to the brain. Anxiety and tension tighten up muscles but the rocking motions loosens them again. So don't feel silly when rocking but understand that it does help to release a little of the pent up nervous energy that is adding to your tension and fear.

TRUST IN YOUR SENSES TO KEEP YOU IN TOUCH WITH REALITY.

*Touch:* The Chinese carve 'worry' objects to handle in times of stress and today you can buy 'eggs' in polished wood, stone or glass that sit comfortably in the hand. Captain Queeg in *The Caine Mutiny* fiddled with a couple of metal balls to relieve his bad temper and stress, much to the annoyance of his officers and crew.

If you are feeling out of touch with reality it helps to touch and finger a specific object. It stops your thoughts concentrating entirely on self and directs them away from your anxiety. When I was agoraphobic I was persuaded by my fiancé to walk up Snowdon with him. He knew nothing about my fears and I felt I had to tackle the climb. I went up barefoot so that the stony ground gave me something to concentrate on. I managed to walk up and down, though I dared not lift my eyes to look about me. I have a photograph of me sitting on a rock gazing at the view below . . . but I was not really looking. When I reached the foot of Snowdon my feet were grazed and bloodied, but they were symbols of my success.

I am not suggesting you try anything as drastic as this, but when you feel really bad, curl up on your bed with a hot-water bottle to cuddle. If you experience 'unreal' feelings, run a hairbrush along the surface of your skin, up and down your arms and lightly across your face. Any tactile stimulation will reassure you that you are still real and will also help to distract you from your anxiety.

Keep a loose elastic band around your wrist, and when you feel panic advancing, snap it soundly. It might just snap *you* back to reality.

Dab an ice cube on the back of your hand and run it over your face. Finger a piece of velvet or satin ribbon and draw it across your cheek like a baby's 'comfort blanket'. If you have a pet to cuddle or stroke this is one of the most therapeutic exercises of all. (If you have a human being to cuddle, even better!)

**Smell:** Few things are more evocative than remembered smells – flowers, perfume, people, cooking odours. Get your imagination working on recalling scents from the past and what you associate them with. Bacon and eggs sizzling in the pan, hospitals, the school classroom, Christmas trees, scents from your childhood how much stronger flowers seemed to smell then. Dettol – doesn't that bring back memories of maternity wards? And how the scent of baby powder makes you recall the time when your children were tiny babies.

Make your memory work for you and take your mind off your anxiety even for a few moments. It will help you concentrate your thoughts on something pleasant. Unpleasant smells can help too – nothing like a bottle of good old-fashioned smelling salts to bring you back to earth with a bump.

You may also try aromatherapy or osmotherapy (see pages 68 and 80 for details).

*Taste:* It helps to suck something bitter or acidic. Sherbert lemons or acid drops get your taste buds operating and the saliva flowing, particularly if your mouth dries up when you feel panicky. Conversely, some people prefer to chew dry biscuits. Very strong peppermints are favoured by a lot of people.

*Sight:* The television is, of course, a boon, though at times it may be difficult to concentrate on the programme. Fish in a tank have always been a therapeutic aid but sometimes expensive to buy and maintain. You can now buy a video of tropical fish swimming about on your TV screen, and there are also other soothing videos – for instance, a blazing, flickering log fire. Cheaper still, if you have a helpful member of the family and access to a video recorder they might make up your own video of favourite subjects – family outings, perhaps.

You could also compile a home video of your favourite television programmes – a cheerful comedy or a soothing nature film. Channel Four has a wonderful series available on video. It is called *Landscapes* and contains breathtakingly beautiful film accompanied by light classical music.

*Colour therapy:* Colour therapy was originally used in ancient Greece and in the healing temples of light and colour at Heliopolis in ancient Egypt. It has also been held in high esteem for thousands of years by the Indians and Chinese. The effects of colour on concentration, performance, sense of physical and mental wellbeing have been well-researched over many years and there is increasing evidence of the therapeutic value of colour in the areas of mental health, hospital recovery rooms and the stimulation of mentally retarded children.

This theory is confirmed by Betty Wood, author of *The Healing Power of Colour*:

Studies in the USA have now established conclusively that our moods are definitely affected by colour. Red, for example, is stimulating and gears up the central nervous system. It can be cheering but is not a relaxing colour and can make people feel uneasy after a time. Greens and blues on the other hand have a sedative effect and make rooms seem more spacious and cool. Yellow is said to lift morale, but can be disturbing. Theo Gimbel, a colour therapist explains: 'The chemical make-up of a person depends on the release of chemicals from the nerve endings of the body. These fine changes can be accelerated or retarded by colour. Some colours help at times of stress, while others definitely increase tension. If you illuminate a room with a particular colour it can do far more good than any tranquillizer or sedative.'

Why not try wearing blue on a bad day, or working with a colour that reflects your mood. If you are really down, try bringing out the watercolours and painting a picture. This could even be considered art therapy, which is a new experience available for panic sufferers.

*Hearing:* An acute sense of hearing can cause problems to the over-sensitive nervous person. First of all there are the noises *inside* your head. Tinnitus, ringing and buzzing in the ears, can be very disturbing, though harmless.

When you are very tense you feel you can hear blood coursing through your veins, hear the thud of your heart beating. Silence is something many people dread so you must counter it with pleasant and reassuring sounds.

Outside yourself repetitive sounds can be very disturbing: a dog barking, water dripping from a tap, the loud ticking of a clock. Further self-help suggestions are:

● Talking to yourself.  No, this is not the first sign of madness, just a way of reassuring yourself. As you finger your comfort object tell yourself that this is helping you on the first steps to recovery. To someone who has not been through this stage it may sound ridiculous and childish, but making a positive affirmation to yourself will guide you through the bad patches

• **Crying.** Dr William Frey, an American researcher at Stanford University, discovered recently that when we cry for emotional reasons our tears contain stress hormones and chemicals associated with stress. Trying to pull yourself together is not the best thing to do. Trying to control your tears may well only suppress the emotions and stress hormones.

Matthew Manning says that in his experience those people who are able to freely express their emotions are far more likely to recover from their illnesses than those who habitually mask their real feelings and never really let go.

• **Music.** The ancient Egyptians called music 'the physic of the soul'. The Persians were said to have cured various illnesses with the sound of the lute. Confucius believed music to be a definite aid to harmonious living and Plato said that health in mind and body could be obtained through music.

In physiological experiments, music has the exact opposite effect to anger on the body. Anger raises the blood pressure – music lowers it. Anger interrupts the flow of gastric juices to the stomach and music aids the digestive processes. Anger causes tension in the muscles – music has a relaxing effect. So play your favourite tapes and records and relax while you listen to them. A 'Walkman' or similar radio cassette player is a real boon to the anxious. Apart from the music, you can play your relaxation and other tapes you find helpful. Radio shows, especially phone-ins, can be a source of comfort, too, particularly in the middle of the night.

*Exercise:* Perhaps you feel you are much too exhausted to contemplate any sort of exercise, but it is important to work off some of that excess nervous energy that has built up inside you, making you feel edgy and jumpy. There is a reason why you might feel uncomfortable when you start to exert yourself because even slight exertion causes the heart to speed up and you become warm and start to sweat. Warning signals flash! Is this the beginning of a panic attack? You scare yourself and start to over-breathe, which makes you feel progressively worse.

191

But gentle exercise can not harm you – it will tone up the body and help to discharge nervous energy.

*Don't* embark on any exercise programme without your doctor's blessing. Concentrate at the moment on gentle walking, swimming, if possible, and even dancing, or just moving to music when you are alone!

*Sleep:* It goes without saying that people prone to anxiety almost certainly have problems sleeping. Bedtime becomes dreadtime for many. It is difficult to sleep when you are screwed up with tension, when unwanted thoughts are continually spinning round in your head.

As always, you are spending much of each day worrying about the following night and also worrying about lack of sleep – whether it is dangerous to go for too long without sleep, how rotten you will feel the next day – and once again you are caught up in the circle of worry/lack of sleep/worry.

Anxiety about sleep loss is itself a common cause of lost sleep. But when we are short of sleep, Nature takes care of us. If we really *need* sleep, we can rely on Nature to ensure we get it. It is not the lack of sleep that makes you feel bad but it is the worry, tension and grinding anxiety that produces the stress. You can not *die* from loss of sleep, nor will you suffer long-term mental or physical ill-effects as a result. You can take comfort from the fact that sleep is a self-regulating system so that when we really need it we will get it and almost nothing will stop us.

Research in California has shown very clearly that sleeping longer than usual, or sleeping at irregular times, can lead to just about the same kinds of inefficiencies, feeling of low spirits and irritability that can be brought about by lack of sleep.

Many anxious people so dread going to bed that they put it off for hours – then they are in such a state and so exhausted they haven't a hope of relaxing into easy sleep. Some people have a sleep phobia, which is often linked with a fear of dying. The actual routine of composing themselves for bed – lying down and waiting for unconsciousnes – is unthinkable. They will sit up all night in a chair and catnap.

Make sure that your bedroom is a welcoming place. Now is the time to break a few rules so that you can get away from feeling that the bedroom is the place where you must lie down and go to sleep. If you turn the light out and close the door, you shut yourself in a 'prison' from which you won't be able to escape until daytime. You can do anything you like to change your surroundings, and if you have a sleeping partner you will just have to persuade him or her that a bedroom 'facelift' is a good idea. A comfortable armchair, portable television, and lots of soothing pictures on the walls will all help.

All too often children are sent to their bedrooms as a punishment and this can instil an aversion to bedtime that may persist through life. If you are not comfortable in your bedroom this will obviously affect your sleep. Have lots of comfortable pillows so you can sit up comfortably and, yes, you can watch television or listen to cassettes or the radio if you wear an earplug so you won't disturb your partner.

Let us touch upon the delicate subject of double beds. Many couples find it impossible to sleep comfortably together but are horrified at the suggestion that they might change to single beds. It is not the beginning of the end as far as the marriage or partnership is concerned; there are quite as many couples sleeping in double beds whose marriages are disasters. Pushing two single beds together is a good solution, and if your partner doesn't like the idea be firm! It is important that your health and wellbeing come before his or her preferred habits.

Try to go to bed at a regular time, and before you do, make an effort to wind down, directing your attention away from the pressures of the day. A hot bath and a warm milky drink may help you to relax. Avoid emotional arguments, excitement and intense mental or physical activity (apart from sex) as the more alert and stimulated you are, the longer it will take you to fall asleep.

If you wake in the night try to relax again before you have time to become alert and start to turn over your problems in your mind. Be disciplined and don't allow yourself the indulgence of thinking. Try not to get agitated about whatever woke you because this will cause your body to release the powerful hormones whose task it is to make you alert and ready for action.

If, after twenty minutes or so, you are still awake and not drowsy, don't fight it. Get up and do something instead of fretting. Make a drink, have something to eat or do something useful. Cool off physically so that when you do go back to your bed it is welcoming and warm. You might feel like going through some relaxation exercises. If you wake around dawn, get up and stay up. The grown-ups aren't going to send you back to bed; you can do what you like.

When you are going through a bad patch you often find it impossible to drop off to sleep as each time you are about to waft away you are startled by a flash of acute panic – your heart races and everything seems unreal. You can't control this but it is not a dangerous symptom so the only way to counteract it is to relax and not let it frighten you. Practise your breathing exercises. If you continually over-breathe – hyperventilate – it makes sense to realize that you can do this even in your sleep.

What happens then? If you are in a light stage of sleep and your breathing is fast and shallow, all the physical symptoms of anxiety build up and you react by having vivid and terrifying dreams. You wake in a state of terror which you attribute to the dreams but, in fact, it is the anxiety which comes first. So you can see how important it is to practise until correct breathing is automatic.

## Keep Going

It is possible for anxiety sufferers to reach a point where they feel that there are so many problems with which to contend there is no point in making further effort. 'You give up and become overwhelmed with the urge to do nothing,' says Dr Neuman in *Fighting Fear*. As time goes on, you do less and less and feel worse and worse. This situation can go on for weeks, months and even years. Other people – your family and friends – say you must want to be like this or else you'd do something about it.

Remember having to write thank-you letters as a child? The longer you left it the more difficult it became and though it was often a case of a few lines, you developed a mental block about it until sometimes the letter never did get written and next year Aunt Ethel left you off her Christmas list.

Dr Neuman says that you may overwhelm yourself into doing nothing and magnify a task to the degree that it seems impossible:

> To illustrate how irrational this is, imagine that every time you sat down to eat, you thought about all the food you would have to eat in your lifetime . . . Just imagine for a moment that piled in front of you are tons of meat, vegetables, fruit, bread and puddings and thousands of gallons of fluids. Now suppose that before every meal you said to yourself 'This meal is just a drop in the ocean. How will I ever get that mountain of food eaten?' When you think about all the things you are putting off you do this very same thing without being aware of it.

'One step at a time' is the motto of the Alcoholics Anonymous Fellowship. You can not concentrate on the day-to-day tasks if you are looking ahead all the time to difficulties you *may* have to face next week.

Too tired to concentrate? Too many thoughts buzzing around in your head and getting out of control? Give yourself something concrete to tackle:

*Lists:* First, find a piece of paper and a pen. Draw up your list. What about? It doesn't matter. Write out a shopping list, make a list of the things you have to do – would like to do – or even the things you did last week.

When it is difficult to face up to the many problems that lurk in the background, the more you try and put them out of your mind the more complex and difficult they become. The reason for making lists is not necessarily to be organized, or for the satisfaction of ticking off items such as 'turn out the kitchen cupboards', or 'clean the oven', when you have actually done it. But List-making gives us the psychological boost of believing that we are in control of our lives.

List-makers are control freaks. Once 'clean the oven', or 'phone Aunt Edith' is written down, the need to actually *do* something about your problems is miraculously let go. Then you have only to tackle just one of them to feel you have made a start.

*Diaries:* Denise wrote to the PAX newsletter to say she was still proceeding by taking two steps forward and one step back:

> It's a bit like snakes and ladders. I amuse myself by getting a notebook and charting my progress each day by drawing a snake or a ladder. An horrendous day can produce a lurid, writhing serpent baring its fangs. One a good day I draw a ladder with the number of rungs demonstrating how much progress I feel I have made. A mediocre day could show a small ladder with just a couple of rungs and perhaps a tiny snake trying to slither up it.
>
> My family is fascinated by my progress book and they say they can now appreciate when I've had a bad day. Daughter Bethan, aged nine, is doing her own snakes and ladders school diary.

Denise's letter illustrates how important it is to keep a record of your progress. Most therapists ask their patients to do this. I know writing things down doesn't come easily to some people and when you are feeling low you may be even less inclined to put pen to paper.

'I don't know what to put,' someone said to me. But it's not that difficult. After all, you could just write, 'Monday, good day Tuesday, rotten day'. But then that's not very positive. Give yourself a target. Don't write, 'Today I am going to walk to the corner' because if you don't make it all the way you will feel you have failed. Wait until the end of the day and look forward to writing, 'Today I reached the corner shop. I felt a bit rocky, but I made it!'

Write something down each day so you can look back and *see* how you have progressed. I was an avid diarist when I was young. Recently I was once again reading pages written forty years ago when I was struggling with severe agoraphobia. I said to my husband, 'I could weep for that girl. I wish I could have given her a glimpse of how good life was going to be later on.'

'You got through those times anyway,' he said.

I'm quite sure those outpourings in my diaries were therapeutic.

I cannot wave a magic wand, or produce a wonder pill to banish all your fears – nobody can do that. I can, however, offer you hope and would remind you once more of the PAX slogan:

TODAY IS THE TOMORROW YOU WORRIED ABOUT YESTERDAY.

# POSTSCRIPT

Whilst working on this book I interviewed a psychiatrist at London's Charing Cross Hospital. We were talking about a new drug which hopefully will prevent panic attacks, at that time undergoing trials. I was asked if I would like to take part in a survey and give details of my own experiences when I suffered from agoraphobia, other phobias and frequent panic attacks. This phobic period lasted from the age of seven to around twenty-seven, though admittedly there was often relief for periods of up to two years.

I filled in the form with my life history. Yes, I remembered my first panic attack very clearly, though I was only seven years old, and yes, I remembered the last severe panic attack which happened when I was going to my office in Whitehall one morning. When did I have the last attack? Thirty-five years ago. The psychiatrist took the form from me and wrote at the bottom, 'In remission'. In remission? Did that mean that he considered my phobic condition was still there buried somewhere in my subconscious, waiting to leap out and strike me down again one day?

I brooded about this over one weekend and it really bothered me. Of course I was completely recovered, I had changed from being nervous, introverted and depressed to being outgoing and able to enjoy life, hadn't I? This was the message I have always been able to pass on to my contacts, particularly the young ones who may feel that they have to face a future filled with fear.

Face panic, float through it. Remain in your phobic situation and don't avoid it, say the experts. And don't rely on crutches. But I relied heavily on my 'props'. My peppermints, my newspaper, any diversionary tactics I could employ. Popping into a telephone box when anxiety began to escalate and always making sure I had enough money for a taxi in case the situation became unbearable, were staples of my existence.

I had been avoiding Westminster for thirty-five years; perhaps I was deluding myself and panic still lurked there, waiting for me to return.

If you have been brought to a full stop by your fears and your lifestyle is affected, you can afford to concentrate on treatment and put behaviour therapy theories into practice; but if you are out in the world, struggling to hold down a job, you can not risk pushing yourself into a phobic situation and facing panic attacks everyday. Sometimes avoidance is necessary if you are going to hold on to a normal life.

If you do suffer a severe panic attack, the feelings and apprehension are further reinforced so you operate at the best level you can, even if you do rely heavily on your props.

You hope the chronic apprehension will gradually die – and it does. Of course, you must know what to do if panic comes, but if you regard it as a nuisance and are not frightened by it you *will* be able to cope.

I decided to face the dreaded spot and see what happened, so on a bright autumn morning I caught a bus up to the centre of London and got off on Westminster Bridge. I stood at the foot of Big Ben and looked up at it – the face seemed to leer as it leaned towards me but I knew that that was due to the inner-ear disorder I have, which makes me feel slightly dizzy when I look upwards. I could ignore that.

I *did* feel apprehensive as I walked into Whitehall and crossed the street, remembering the times when I had to get a taxi to go around Parliament Square – about a quarter of a mile. The sun was shining on the Houses of Parliament and I continued to walk round the square – twice. I stopped and chatted to overseas visitors who are always eager to talk. No nervous feelings, no apprehension.

Of course, it had all gone.

# RECOMMENDED READING

*Agoraphobia.* Vose, Ruth Hurst, Faber & Faber Ltd, 1981.

*Acupuncture, Cure of Many Diseases.* Mann, Felix; Pan Books Ltd, 1978.

*Agoraphobia: Coping with the World Outside.* Frampton, Muriel; Turnstone Press Ltd, 1984.

*Agoraphobia: Simple, Effective Treatment.* Weekes, Claire; Angus & Robertson, 1977.

*Aromatherapy for Women.* Tisserand, Maggie; Thorsons Ltd, 1985.

*Being Happy!* Matthews, Andrew; In Books, Media Masters Pte. Ltd., 1988.

*Coming off Tranquillizers and Sleeping Pills.* Trickett, Shirley; Thorsons Ltd, 1986.

*The Doctor's Vitamin and Mineral Encyclopaedia.* Hindler, Dr Sheldon Saul, M.D., Ph.D.; Arrow Books, 1991.

*The Family Guide to Homoeopathy.* Lockie, Dr Andrew; Penguin Books, 1989.

*Fears and Phobias.* Marks, Isaac M.; William Heinemann Medical Books, 1969.

*Feel The Fear and Do It Anyway.* Jeffers, Susan; Arrow Books, 1991.

*Fighting Fear.* Neuman, Dr Fredric; David & Charles, 1986.

*Gestalt Therapy.* Perls, Frederick; Crown, New York, 1951.

*Healing without Harm.* Bartlett, E. G.; Eliot Right Way Books, 1987.

*Heaven's Breath, A Natural History of the Wind.* Watson, Lyall; Hodder & Stoughton, 1984.

*Herbal Medicine.* Buchman, Dian; Rider, 1987.

*Living with Fear, Understanding and Coping with Anxiety.* Marks, Isaac M; McGraw-Hill Book Company, 1978.

*Matthew Manning's Guide to Self Healing.* Manning, Matthew; Thorsons Ltd, 1989.

*Mind to Mind.* Shine, Betty; Transworld, 1989.

*Mind Magic.* Shine, Betty; Transworld, 1991.

*Not All in the Mind.* Mackarness, Richard; Pan Books Ltd, 1976.

*Obsessional Thoughts and Behaviour.* Toates, Dr Frederick; Thorsons, 1990.

*Other Lives, Other Selves.* Woolger, Roger J.; Crucible, part of Thorsons, 1987.

*Peace from Nervous Suffering.* Weekes, Claire; Pan Books Ltd, 1976.

*Phobia: The Facts.* Goodwin, Dr Donald W.; Oxford University Press, 1983.

*Phobia Free.* Levinson, Harold, N., M. D., with Steven Carter; M. Evans and Co. Inc., New York 1986.

*Phobias.* Mitchell, Dr Ross.; Pelican Books, 1982.

*Phobias and Obsessions.* Melville, Joy; George Allen & Unwin, 1977.

*The Reflexology Handbook.* Norman, Laura; with Thomas Cowan; Judy Piatkus, 1989.

*Self Help For Your Nerves.* Weekes, Claire; Angus & Robertson, 1969.

*Smile Therapy.* Hodgkinson, Liz; Macdonald and Co., 1987.

*Taking the Fear Out of Flying.* Yaffé, Dr Maurice; David & Charles, 1987.

*The Myth of Neurosis, A Case for Moral Therapy.* Wood, Garth; Macmillan London, 1983.

*The Tranquillizer Trap.* Melville, Joy; Fontana, 1984.

*Well Woman Self Help Directory.* Bradford, Nikki; Sidgwick & Jackson, 1990.

*Who's Afraid of Agoraphobia?* Neville, Alice; Arrow Books, 1986.

# HELPFUL ORGANIZATIONS

## PHOBIAS AND ANXIETY DISORDERS

There are a number of phobia organizations and self-help groups, but many rise and fall so quickly that any list would be out of date by the time this book is published. This is usually due to financial problems, I'm afraid.

Please contact PAX for latest information about such groups.

PAX is an information service for those suffering from panic attacks, anxiety disorders and phobias. There is a bi-monthly newsletter, including contact lists and up-to-date information about therapies available. Cassettes available include: 'Who's Afraid of Agoraphobia?', 'Panic Attacks' and 'Who's Afraid of the Dentist?' For free information pack please send a large stamped self-addressed envelope to PAX, 4 Manorbrook, Blackheath, London SE3 9AW.

The following organizations will provide some helpful advice. Always remember to send a self-addressed stamped envelope when making enquiries.

Action Against Allergy
43, The Downs, London SW20 8HG

Association for Post-Natal Illness
7 Gowan Avenue, London SW6 6RH

Association of Qualified Curative Hypnotherapists
10 Balaclava Road, Kings Heath, Birmingham B14 7SG

Bach Flower Remedies

Dr Edward Bach, Mount Vernon, Sotwell, Wallingford, Oxon
OX10 0PZ

British Acupuncture Register and Directory
34 Alderney Street, London SW1 4VE

British Association for Counselling
37A Sheep Street, Rugby CV21 3BX

British Council for Complementary and Alternative Medicine
Suite One, 19A Cavendish Square, London W1M 9AD

British Dental Association
63 Wimpole Street, London W1

British Homoeopathic Association
BMA House, Tavistock Square, London WC1H 9JP

British Hypnotherapy Association
67 Upper Berkeley Street, London W1H 7DH

British Medical Association
BMA House, Tavistock Square, London WC1H 9JP

British Society of Medical and Dental Hypnosis
c/o Ms M. Samuels, 42 Links Road, Ashtead, Surrey KT21 2HJ

British Wheel of Yoga
1 Hamilton Place, Boston Road, Sleaford, Lincs

Centre for Developmental Learning Difficulties Ltd.
The Burrs, Church Road, Iver Heath, Bucks SLO 0RD
For details of Neuro-Developmental Remediation – a highly
successful approach to addressing specific learning difficulties
in children and young adults.

Church Council for Health and Healing
Marylebone Road, London NW1 5LT

Council for Acupuncture
Suite One, 19A Cavendish Place, London W1M 9AD

Council for Involuntary Tranquillizer Addiction (CITA)
(051) 949 9192
Helpline, advice line and telephone counselling available every
weekday between 10a.m and 5.30p.m.

Dental Health Foundation

Eastlands Court, St Peter's Road, Rugby, Warwickshire CV21 3GP

Dietary Therapy Society
33 Priory Gardens, London N6 5QU

Drugs Release
169 Commercial Street, London E1 3BW

Institute for Complementary Medicine
21 Portland Place, London W1N 3AF

The Institute for Optimum Nutrition
5 Jerdan Place, London SW6 1BE

Institute for Neuro-Physiological Psychology
c/o Dr Peter Blythe, Warwick House, 4 Stanley Place, Chester, Cheshire
For details and advice on Neuro-Developmental Delay (NDD)

International Institute of Reflexology
28 Hollyfield Avenue, London N11 3BY

ISDD (Institute for the Study of Drug Dependence)
1–4 Hatton Place, Hatton Garden, London EC1N 8NP

Matthew Manning Centre
33 Buryfields, Cage End, Hatfield Broad Oak, Bishops Stortford, Herts CR2 7HT

MIND (National Association for Mental Health)
22 Harley Street, London W1N 2ED

National Association for Pre-Menstrual Tension
PO Box 72, Sevenoaks, Kent TA13 1XQ

National Federation of Spiritual Healers
Old Manor Farm Studio, Sunbury-on-Thames, Middlesex TW16 6RG

National Institute of Medical Herbalists
41 Hatherly Road, Winchester, Hants SO22 6RR

Neural-Developmental Delay (NDD) Support Group
PO Box 1018, Iver, Bucks SLO 0SA

Pre-Menstrual Tension Advisory Service (now the Woman's Nutritional Advisory Service)

PO Box 268, Hove, East Sussex BN3 1RW

Psychotherapy Centre
67 Upper Berkeley Street, London W1N 2ED

Rainbow Foundation
c/o Annette Smith, Rainbow Foundation Head Office,
27 South Road, Hartlepool, Cleveland TS26 9HB
The first national support group for NDD (Neuro-Developmental Delay) sufferers.

RELATE
Herbert Gray College, Little Church Street, Rugby CV21 3AP

RELEASE
169 Commercial Street, London E1 3BW
For information about prescription drugs.

Relaxation for Living
29 Burwood Park Road, Walton-on-Thames, Surrey KY12 5LH
Send large SAE for information about relaxation classes, correspondence courses, leaflets, books and cassettes, including those recorded by Dr Claire Weekes.

Samaritans
17 Uxbridge Road, Slough, Bucks (See telephone directory for local branches)

Shiatsu Society
c/o Elaine Liechti, 19 Longside Park, Kilbarchan, Renfrewshire PA10 2EP

Society of Holistic Practitioners
Old Hall, East Bergholt, Colchester CO7 6TG

Society of Homoeopaths
2 Artisan Road, Northampton NN1 4HU

Terence Higgins Trust
52–54 Gray's Inn Road, London WC1X 8JU

Tisserand Aromatherapy Institute
10 Victoria Grove, Second Avenue, Hove, East Sussex BN3 2IJ

Yoga for Health Foundation
Ickwell Bury, Northill, Biggleswade, Bedfordshire SG18 9ED

# INDEX